FINANCE

ACT 1990

FINANCE

ACT 1990

A GUIDE

A commentary on the complex changes to taxation
introduced by the Finance Act 1990

Ernst & Young

KOGAN
PAGE

First published in 1990

Kogan Page Limited
120 Pentonville Road
London N1 9JN

© Ernst & Young, September 1990

British Library Cataloguing in Publication Data

A CIP record for this book is available from the British Library

ISBN 0-7494-0255-5

Printed and bound in Great Britain by
Biddles Ltd, Guildford and Kings Lynn

FOREWORD

As National Tax Publications Partner, I am very pleased to introduce the first booklet from the Ernst & Young tax practice which is available both to our clients and to the general public.

The Finance Act 1990 received the Royal Assent on 26 July 1990 giving legislative effect to the Chancellor's Budget proposals announced on 20 March 1990. Some significant changes have also been introduced since the Budget including provisions relating to motor mileage allowances and port privatisation.

In the personal sphere, the Budget measures now contained in the Act include the introduction of relief on workplace nurseries, the gift aid scheme, TESSA (the tax-exempt special savings account), and the abolition of composite rate tax and of stamp duty on shares. For corporate taxpayers, relief has been introduced for the incorporation of branches but there is further complexity for dual-resident companies and the regime surrounding convertible and indexed securities. All companies will be affected by new administrative provisions relating to 'pay and file' expected to take effect in 1993, and banks, building societies and particularly life assurance companies are specifically affected by major changes applicable to their industries.

The aim in providing this commentary is to outline the contents of the Act and give assistance in the interpretation of provisions which inevitably make the tax aspects of our business activities more complex. Our understanding of the provisions is stated as clearly and accurately as possible but without overburdening the reader with too much detail. And rather than follow the order of sections and schedules contained in the Act, the book has been designed for the reader to be able to find and comprehend more easily the topic in which he or she may be interested.

For these reasons, the book is not intended to answer every question which arises in practice and it is recommended that specific advice be sought on any particular matter before action is taken.

In conclusion, I would like to thank the many partners and staff from the various specialist tax departments of Ernst & Young who have contributed their time and the benefit of their experience to this publication. As a result, we hope readers will find this guide a most authoritative publication on the Finance Act 1990 and, above all, of practical use now and in the future.

Laurence Bard
September 1990

TABLE OF CONTENTS

ABBREVIATIONS

ABA	Agricultural buildings allowance
ACT	Advance corporation tax
AVC	Additional voluntary contribution
BES	Business expansion scheme
Board	Board of Inland Revenue
CA	Capital allowance
CAA 90	Capital Allowances Act 1990
CGT	Capital gains tax
CGTA	Capital Gains Tax Act 1979
CIC	Close investment-holding company
CRT	Composite rate tax
CT	Corporation tax
Customs	Customs & Excise
DSS	Department of Social Security
DTI	Department of Trade and Industry
EC	European Community
EEIG	European Economic Interest Grouping
ESC	Extra-statutory concession
ESOP	Employee share ownership trust
FA	Finance Act, e.g. FA 1989
FII	Franked investment income
FSA	Financial Services Act
IBA	Industrial buildings allowance
IHT	Inheritance tax
IHTA	Inheritance Tax Act 1984
IRPR	Inland Revenue press release
IT	Income tax
NIC	National insurance contribution
PAYE	Pay as you earn
PRP	Profit-related pay
PRT	Petroleum Revenue Tax
QUEST	Qualifying employee share ownership trust
Revenue	Inland Revenue
RPI	Retail prices index
S	Section
Sch	Schedule

SI	Statutory Instrument
SIB	Securities and Investments Board
SP	Statement of practice
TA	Income and Corporation Taxes Act 1988
TA70	Income and Corporation Taxes Act 1970
TESSA	Tax-exempt special savings account
TMA	Taxes Management Act 1970
UCITS	Undertakings for collective investment in transferable securities
USM	Unlisted securities market
VAT	Value added tax
VATA	Value Added Tax Act 1983

1 VALUE ADDED TAX
REGISTRATION

General
S.10

From 21 March 1990 the rules on VAT registration limits have been radically changed. The changes are essentially a simplification measure aimed at helping the smaller business. The quarterly turnover limit has gone; so too has the need to anticipate future taxable income over the next year. But in their place there is a requirement to view past and future taxable turnover at, at least, monthly intervals.

Someone making taxable supplies but not registered becomes liable to registration:

a) at the end of any month if taxable supplies in the last year have exceeded £25,400; *or*

b) immediately if it is likely that taxable supplies in the next 30 days will exceed £25,400.

Where the monthly rule in a) above applies, Customs must be notified within 30 days of the end of the relevant month. Registration is then normally from the end of the month following the relevant month unless an earlier date is agreed. Where an immediate liability arises under b) above, Customs are to be told before the end of the 30 day period; but there is no possibility of deferment, as was the case previously, of the date from which registration is effected.

Where the business becomes registrable under both a) and b) above, the date of registration is determined by the rules for b).

Business transfers
S.10 (2)

Further simplification measures concern transfers of businesses as going concerns. Again having effect from 21 March 1990, the transferee of a business becomes liable to be registered at the time of transfer if:

a) his taxable supplies in the last year have exceeded £25,400; *or*

b) it is likely that his taxable supplies in the next 30 days will exceed £25,400.

The effect of Section 33(1)(a) VATA is to treat as the transferee's taxable supplies those previously made by the transferor from the same business. Thus, for the purposes of a) above the transferee will need to take these supplies into account in addition to any taxable supplies actually made by him before the transfer date. Notification in either event is required within 30 days, although, if Customs are satisfied that taxable supplies in the following year will not exceed £24,400, registration may be excused. If there is a liability to be registered, registration will take effect from the transfer date.

Customs apparently intend these rules to be applied to transfers of part of a business as they apply to transfers of the whole of a business.

Deregistration   Although not contained in the Finance Act as such, the limit of taxable supplies for deregistration purposes was also increased, in this case by Treasury Order. From 1 June 1990 a person may ask to be deregistered if it is likely, and Customs are satisfied, that taxable supplies in the following year will not exceed £24,400.

2 VALUE ADDED TAX
BAD DEBT RELIEF

S.11 From 1 April 1991 there is to be a more comprehensive VAT bad debt relief. No longer is it to be dependent on the formal insolvency of the debtor. Instead, a person may claim a refund of the VAT element of an outstanding debt where:

a) the original supply took place on or after 1 April 1989 and was for a consideration in money the VAT on which has been accounted for;

b) the whole or part of the consideration has been written off in his accounts; *and*

c) two years have passed since the supply was made.

For the purposes of a) and c) above the normal tax point rules apply.

Where part of a debt has been paid, relief will only be given by reference to the balance outstanding. In no case, however, will a refund be given where the consideration for a supply was above open market value or where, in the case of a supply of goods, property has not passed. Goods sold under reservation of title (i.e. by contract containing a 'Romalpa' clause) will consequently require the formal waiver of any rights under that clause. To the extent that payment of a debt previously written off is subsequently received, regulations will require repayment of a proportion of the amount refunded.

The new rules are intended to replace, rather than supplement, the existing bad debt relief in Section 22 VATA and the VAT (Bad Debt Relief) Regulations 1986. Section 22 will continue to be available for debts arising before 26 July 1990; however, where relief is claimed under Section 22, it will not also be available under the new provisions. This will be important since, for a claim under Section 22 to be entertained, the creditor must prove in the insolvency for only the 'net of VAT' amount — i.e. his entitlement to the VAT element must be foregone.

As with the existing Section 22 relief, much of the detail is to be left to regulations. These have yet to be issued. They will, in particular, cover:

- the timing, form and manner of claims; also evidence and records required;

- stipulations as to refunds in appropriate cases;

- rules for determining whether, when and to what extent consideration is to be taken as written off; *and*

- rules for determining how a payment received is to be treated both in arriving at the amount outstanding on the original debt and in relation to amounts previously written off.

3 DOMESTIC ACCOMMODATION

S.12   From 26 July 1990, VAT on goods or services acquired or imported by a company does not rank as input VAT to the extent that they are used or to be used in providing domestic accommodation for a director of the company or those connected with him. The meaning of a company, of a director and those connected with him broadly follow definitions used for direct tax purposes.

The measures are aimed at giving effect to the intention of the EC Sixth VAT Directive and bring the treatment of directors' accommodation into line with that provided for partners and sole proprietors. The rules for other directors' expenditure and for expenditure relating to employees remain unaltered.

4 | SUPPLIES TO GROUPS

S.14 From April 1990 there is a change in the treatment of businesses acquired on a VAT free basis by a partly exempt VAT group. Section 29A VATA, whilst not affecting the transferor, creates a deemed self-supply of the chargeable assets of a business acquired by such a group on a going concern basis. By concession, this does not extend to goodwill; Customs also have power to reduce a charge where full input VAT relief has not been enjoyed by the transferor.

The effect of the change is to exclude from the charge to VAT any assets subject to the Capital Goods Scheme. This scheme applies to partly exempt businesses acquiring on or after 1 April 1990:

- computers and items of computer equipment costing individually £50,000 or more

- land and buildings (including extensions) which have been subject to VAT on a value of £250,000 or more

and requires adjustments to input VAT relief over a five-year period for computers; and ten years for land and buildings. Where there is a transfer of a business on a going concern basis, the transferor makes no final adjustment; instead, adjustments are required to be made by the transferee for the remainder of the five or ten year period. The change thus prevents what would otherwise be an element of double taxation.

5 VALUE ADDED TAX
CHARITIES

The 1990 Budget extended the zero rating available for certain supplies by or to charities or purchased out of charitable funds. The measures are not contained in the Finance Act but are to be found in two Treasury Orders laid before Parliament on 21 March 1990; both came into force on 1 May 1990.

The VAT (Transport) Order 1990

The existing relief afforded in Item 3 Group 10 Schedule 5 VATA to the RNLI for the supply of lifeboats, launching and recovery equipment and for the modification, repair and maintenance of slipways is now given to other similar charities. The Item is also extended to cover the construction of new slipways, which became taxable at the standard rate from 1 April 1990.

VAT (Charities) Order 1990

Group 16 Schedule 5 VATA also zero rates certain supplies of goods purchased from charitable funds or voluntary contributions when intended for use by eligible bodies such as Health Authorities, charitable hospitals, hospices and rescue or first aid services. From 1 May 1990 the range of goods to which the provisions apply is increased; greater emphasis is also given to the use to which the goods are put rather than to their description. In addition, relief is given to airborne and waterborne, as well as ordinary, ambulances.

Similar relief is at the same time given to preparatory services related to printed media advertising; also to the sale of donated goods by a trading subsidiary owned by a charity to which all of its profits are covenanted and where the charity is established primarily for the relief of distress or the protection or benefit of animals. The donation of goods for sale or export by such a company is equally now zero rated.

6 VALUE ADDED TAX
OTHER VAT CHANGES

S. 13 From 26 July 1990 there is a restriction in the export relief for goods supplied for use as stores on a foreign-going voyage or flight. From that date zero rating is not available where the voyage or flight is undertaken for private purposes. Supplies for normal commercial voyages or flights are unaffected; so too is any zero rating under other provisions, e.g. as food.

S. 15 Consequent on the changes to the VAT bad debt relief, there are further changes to the powers of Customs to assess VAT wrongly repaid or credited. From 26 July 1990 Customs can, in particular, assess where bad debt relief has been claimed and subsequently the debt (or part of the debt) has been paid without the VAT element being reimbursed. The change does, however, appear to have a wider effect; it may, for example, extend to cases where, say, input VAT or output VAT has been accounted for on the basis of estimates the agreement for which has been founded on a misunderstanding or misrepresentation of the facts.

S. 16 Again from 26 July 1990 there is a change to the rules allowing Customs to charge a commercial rate of interest on underpaid VAT (default interest). The change is intended to link in with the facility for annual accounting available to traders with a taxable turnover under £250,000.

7 INCOME TAX
RATES AND ALLOWANCES

S.17   The basic rate of income tax remains at 25% for the year 1990/91. The higher rate also remains at 40% and there has been no change in the threshold which remains at £20,700.

Personal allowances SI 1990/677 S.18   The main income tax allowances have been increased by 7.7% rounded up in line with the statutory indexation provisions. The blind person's allowance has, however, been doubled to £1,080.

The allowances which will apply for 1990/91 are detailed in the Appendix.

Other reliefs S.71   There is no change for 1990/91 in the £30,000 limit on mortgage loans, the interest on which qualifies for tax relief.

Car benefits S.22   Car scale charges have been increased by 20% for 1990/91, but the separate scales for fuel benefit have not. Details are shown in the Appendix.

S.82   This provision amends the legislation relating to income arising to minors from parental settlements. Income paid to or for the benefit of the child (or deemed to be so) is aggregable with that of the parent. The de minimis exception is raised from £5 to £100 per annum with effect for the 1991/92 tax year.

8 CARE FOR CHILDREN

Hitherto, the provision by an employer of any child care facilities, like other benefits in kind, was chargeable on employees earning more than £8,500 per annum (including the value of taxable benefits) as a benefit equal to the cost to the employer, less any amount made good by the employee.

S. 21 From 6 April 1990, the provision of work place nurseries and other child care by an employer may now be exempt.

The provision of care for an employee's child under the age of 18 is an exempt benefit if:

- the child is a child for whom the employee has parental responsibility, is resident with the employee, or is a child of the employee and maintained at his expense;

- the care, which means any form of care or supervised activity (and need not be provided on a regular basis), is not provided on premises used wholly or mainly as a domestic dwelling;

- *either* the employer alone makes available the premises, in which case the employer need take no further part in the conduct or management of the child care arrangements;

  or, the employer will in conjunction with others, participate in arrangements for the provision of child care, and will be responsible either alone or in conjunction with them for financing and managing the child care arrangements. In these cases, the employer need not provide the accommodation but it must be provided by other participants in the arrangements;

- any requirement for registration either of premises (under S.1 Nurseries and Child-Minders Regulation Act 1948 or S.11 Children and Young Persons Act (Northern Ireland) 1968) or of any person providing the care (under S.71 Children Act 1989) is met.

Where the employer does not make the premises available then he must participate in the child care arrangements including their financing and management. This is intended to ensure that bookings for employees' children at commercial nurseries are excluded, but the degree of participation required by the employer in the management of such arrangements is unclear. As a minimum it would appear that the employer should be represented on any executive body or committee responsible for overseeing the arrangements.

The local authority registering the facility may require that meals be provided. While it is not clear whether the definition of child care extends to the provision of meals and other facilities (including clothing, toys, outings, etc) which would otherwise be assessable as benefits on the child's parent employee, it is assumed that it will be exempt.

Child care falling within the exemption does not include supervised activity provided primarily for educational purposes; this rule is necessary to exclude from the exemption the provision of subsidised schooling by the employer. It is considered that nursery education will not be excluded because the primary purpose of the employer will be to provide for child care, rather than (non-compulsory) educational facilities.

Revenue statements make clear that the exemption is intended to apply to nurseries run at the work place, or elsewhere by the employer, and to nurseries run by employers in joint ventures with other employers, local authorities or voluntary organisations. Provided that it is the employer who makes available the premises, child care can be provided by individuals or organisations wholly unconnected with the employer, and payments made by the employer under contracted arrangements to such individuals or organisations fall within the exemption. The making available of premises appears to include the provision of premises already occupied by the employer, or acquired by him for the purpose of provision of child care facilities, or the hiring of premises (such as a hall) for this purpose. However, local authority conditions for those under age five are likely to contain rules which may exclude certain halls (eg church halls).

Cash allowances provided by an employer, or payment of an employee's bills for child care continue to be chargeable to tax (and subject to PAYE and National Insurance contributions). The provision of vouchers by an employer which can be used by the employee to meet child care expenses also continues to be chargeable. All employees, irrespective of their level of earnings remain subject to tax on such benefits.

9 INCOME TAX
CHARITABLE GIVING

Payroll deduction scheme
S.24

The limit for donations to charity under the payroll deduction scheme has been increased from £480 per annum to £600 per annum with effect for 1990/91. The scheme, introduced in FA 1986, enables charitable donations within the specified annual limit to be deducted as expenses incurred in the year of assessment from Schedule E earnings, provided that the payments are not intended to fulfil any prior obligations of the donor under a deed of covenant. The provisions enable immediate relief from higher rate tax to be given as employers deduct the gifts from pay before applying PAYE.

Gift aid
S.25

The introduction of the payroll deduction scheme was intended to encourage and facilitate charitable giving, which would otherwise have required the formality of a deed of covenant to attract tax relief. The Finance Act further seeks to extend the tax efficiency of charitable gifts by the introduction of the Gift Aid scheme to apply to gifts on or after 1 October 1990. Donors under this new scheme will attract higher rate tax relief on single gifts of a minimum of £600 per annum and gifts not exceeding in aggregate £5 million per annum. Although from the minimum level it appears that the intention is to dovetail with the payroll giving scheme, this is not quite the case since the latter contemplates a maximum gross gift of £600 whilst the new provision contemplates a minimum net gift of £600 (a gross equivalent of £800).

Gift Aid will apply to UK resident individuals only, bringing the position into line with the corporate provisions introduced by FA 86 in relation to single gifts. Payment will be treated as made net of basic rate tax as with covenants, the charity reclaiming that tax from the Revenue, and the donor securing higher rate tax relief. Again, as with covenants, payment must be made out of taxed income or the donor must account to the Revenue for basic rate tax. The Revenue are to prescribe an appropriate form of certificate for completion to the effect that the gift satisfies the various qualifying criteria set out in the legislation.

For example:

	£	£
Single gift of £800 gross − cash paid	600	600
Tax deducted (25%)	200	
Charity receives	800	
Individual reclaims higher rate (15%)		(120)
Cost of gift to individual		480

Only gifts of cash qualify, and it is not possible to obtain relief for bequests made by the donor on his or her death. Further conditions require that the donor receives no benefit (subject to a de minimis exception) in return for the gift and that there is no property purchase from the donor (or connected persons) associated with it. The de minimis value of permissible benefit is set at 2½% of the value of the gift or £250, whichever is the lesser figure.

S.94 Section 94 of the Finance Act introduces the power for the Revenue to require production of books, documents and other records in the possession or control of the charity which contain information relating to payments made under the above provision (and the equivalent corporate provision: see *30: Company gifts*) in respect of which tax repayment claims have been made.

The above conditions are intended to counter exploitation of the new Gift Aid reliefs since the upper limit of £5m could potentially encourage the development of complex schemes to take advantage of the beneficial fiscal position. The government has sought to balance the position as between those with genuine donative intent, whom they wish to encourage by financial incentives to giving, and what they view as abuse, through the use of private charities in circumstances where they remain unconvinced of the paramount charitable objective.

IRPR SP4/90
20 March 1990 The new provisions go hand in hand with a clarification by the Revenue of the existing position with regard to covenanted donations. Failure to comply with the legal formalities in relation to covenants, often through a lack of appreciation of the requirements, has meant that in the past charities have been dependent on the practices adopted by their Inspector as to the tax effectiveness of particular donations. That position was unsatisfactory and the guidance now given by the Revenue in their Press Release provides a clear framework within which the charity can operate together with draft documentation which the Revenue consider to be acceptable.

10

TAX-EXEMPT SPECIAL SAVINGS ACCOUNTS (TESSAs)

S. 28   With effect from 1 January 1991, banks and building societies will be able to operate 'tax exempt special savings accounts' (TESSA) on which, subject to certain conditions and regulations, any interest or bonus for a period of five years will be disregarded for all tax purposes.

Conditions   An account will be a TESSA if:

- the account is opened on or after 1 January 1991 by an individual aged 18 or more;

- the account is identified as a TESSA with a building society or authorised bank (which is not prohibited from operating TESSAs) and is not connected with any other account held by the account holder or any other person;

- the account is not a joint account or an account held on behalf of another person;

- the account meets any conditions to be prescribed in Regulations to be made by the Board;

- the account holder does not simultaneously hold any other TESSA account with the same or any other building society or bank.

Loss of exemption   Provided these conditions continue to be met an account will continue to be a TESSA for five years from the date it is opened. However, it will cease to qualify as a TESSA on the death of the account holder or if any of the following events occur:

- the limits on deposits are exceeded.

    During the first 12 months an account is open, a maximum of £3,000 can be deposited.

    During any subsequent period of 12 months not more than £1,800 can be deposited. In total not more than £9,000 can be deposited in the account.

- the limits on withdrawals are exceeded.

Deposits into the account cannot be withdrawn until the fifth anniversary of the opening of the account (or the earlier death of the account holder) without loss of the tax exempt status. Interest or any bonus on the account can be withdrawn although an amount equal to income tax at the basic rate in force at the time payment is made must be retained in the account.

- the TESSA account holder cannot assign any rights in respect of the accounts or use the account as security for a loan.

Income tax charge If an account ceases to be a tax exempt account before the fifth anniversary of the opening of the account (or before the death of the account holder), the aggregate interest or bonus earned on the account will be subject to income tax in the year in which the account ceased to be tax exempt.

TESSA regulations The Board may make Regulations covering additional conditions necessary for maintaining TESSA accounts including information to be provided by building societies and banks and arrangements for the transfer of a TESSA from one building society or bank to another.

11 INCOME TAX
COMPOSITE RATE TAX

S. 30 & Sch. 5 The legislation dealing with the abolition of composite rate tax (CRT) takes effect with regard to interest credited on or after 6 April 1991.

At present, financial institutions account to the Revenue for a fixed rate of tax on interest paid to depositors. That rate is less than the basic rate of tax (for 1990/91 being 22%) but full credit for basic rate is given to depositors against their tax liability. However, no tax refunds are made against CRT paid. The new provisions impose an obligation to deduct basic rate tax which will be fully reclaimable, where appropriate. Taxation will be on income arising in the current year of assessment and not the preceding year.

The abolition of CRT will benefit those with smaller incomes and unused allowances who would otherwise have been unable to reclaim the tax. The advent of independent taxation from 6 April 1990 has greatly increased the number of investors potentially within this net. However, with the increased tax rate it is likely that the net rate of return to the tax paying investor will suffer.

From 6 April 1991 the new rules are to apply to interest paid by building societies, banks, local authorities and other deposit takers. Basic rate tax will be deducted from interest at source, higher rate tax being assessed separately as appropriate, and tax repayments being made upon the relevant claims. The detailed provisions are to be set out in regulations made by the Revenue.

It is intended to introduce regulations allowing account holders (or, if different, the persons beneficially entitled to the funds) who are not likely to be liable to income tax, to so certify, enabling payment to be made gross and obviating the necessity to make repayment claims.

(For further detail of these provisions see *40: Banks and building societies*).

12 | INCOME TAX
BUSINESS EXPANSION SCHEME

Locality rule
S. 73

Under FA 88, BES relief is available for investments made in shares in companies whose activities consist of providing private rented housing. The Act specifically excludes expensive dwellings. For this purpose an expensive dwelling is one which at any time within four years of the relevant date has a market value which exceeded £125,000 in Greater London or £85,000 elsewhere.

Market value is defined as the price which, at the relevant date, it might reasonably have been expected to fetch in a sale on the open market. The relevant date means the later of the date of issue of the shares or the date the company acquired the dwelling house. In arriving at this value it is to be assumed that the dwelling house was in the same state as it was at the valuation date and the locality in which it is situated was also in the same state and had the same services and facilities as applied at the valuation date.

Where the valuation date is on or after 20 March 1990 the 'locality rule' will no longer apply. With effect from that date, dwellings will not now be excluded from the scheme if their value increases above the limits simply as a result of improvements to the services and facilities in their locality.

Limit on the
amount of finance
SI 1990/862

Section 290A TA 88 imposes a limit on the amount a BES company can raise on which BES relief is due. This limit has been increased from £500,000 to £750,000 for share issues on or after 1 May 1990.

Other amendments
Sch. 14 para 17

Two amendments have been made to correct errors arising from the consolidation of legislation into TA 88. The first is that the CGT exemption applies only where BES relief is given to the person making the disposal. This is deemed always to have had effect.

The second is that the provision dealing with the exchange of shares on company reconstructions, etc when BES relief is withdrawn only applies to eligible BES shares issued after 18 March 1986. An individual may elect that this amendment should not have effect with respect to exchanges, etc which took place before 1 January 1990. Such an election is irrevocable and must be made before 6 April 1991. If no election is made the amendment is deemed always to have had effect.

13 | INCOME TAX
OTHER SAVINGS CHANGES

Pension scheme earnings cap SI 1990/679

The permitted maximum of an employee's remuneration for the purposes of pension contributions is increased to £64,800 for the year 1990/91. The corresponding figure for 1988/89 and 1989/90 was £60,000. This amendment was made by Statutory Instrument.

Extension of save as you earn (SAYE) accounts S. 29

The exemption from income tax and capital gains tax on any terminal bonus or interest payable under a certified contractual saving scheme hitherto has only been available on SAYE contracts operated by the Department of National Savings and building societies. With effect from 26 July 1990, the exemption will be extended to enable authorised banks to operate SAYE contracts.

The current limits on monthly savings under an SAYE contract are £10 minimum and £150 maximum.

Personal equity plans (PEPs) SI 1990/678

The annual investment limit in personal equity plans is with effect from 6 April 1990 increased from £4,800 to £6,000 of which £3,000 may be in unit or investment trusts. The requirement that such trusts must have invested at least 75% in UK equities is to be reduced to 50%. If a trust does not meet this requirement, the maximum investment through a PEP will be £900.

Friendly societies S. 49

The limit on premiums for tax exempt life and endowment policies offered by friendly societies is increased from £100 to £150 per annum with effect from 1 September 1990.

14 INCOME TAX
BUSINESS DEDUCTIONS

Ss. 75 & 76   Contributions to a training and enterprise council (TEC) or a local enterprise company (LEC) are deductible in arriving at the profit of any trade, profession or vocation if made on or after 1 April 1990 and before 1 April 1995. An identical relief to that for TECs and LECs already applies for contributions to Local Enterprise Agencies and that relief is now extended to contributions made before 1 April 1995. See *29: Contributions to LEAs, TECs and LECs* for further details.

S. 78   Expenditure incurred after 6 April 1989 on the restoration or preparation of a waste disposal site qualifies for deduction from trading profits. See *44: Waste Disposal* for further details.

S. 88   A number of technical amendments are made to CAA 1990 which restore this consolidated legislation to the provisions contained in the original enactments.

15 | MOTOR MILEAGE ALLOWANCES

From 6 April 1990, employees using their own cars on business will be affected by three changes, two to the law and one to an administrative scheme (the Fixed Profit Car Scheme, or FPCS) run by the Inland Revenue. The changes relate to mileage allowances, capital allowances and interest relief, and were announced by means of a Press Release dated 21 June, 1990.

Fixed profit car scheme
IRPR 21.6.90

The FPCS is a voluntary scheme for taxing mileage allowances. Each year the employee's taxable mileage 'profit' is calculated by reference to the excess of the rate of the mileage allowance received over the FPCS 'tax-free' rates detailed below. Up to 1989/90 an employer could pay, tax free, either a flat-rate mileage allowance of up to 30p per mile to all employees using their own cars, or allowances linked to engine size.

The Revenue now considers that these rates were too generous and involved a profit element for the 'high mileage' employee. The rates have been revised to ensure that they no more than cover the cost, including depreciation, of the business use of the car.

The main changes are that:

* the old rates will only apply to business mileage of up to 4000 miles a year;

* much lower rates will apply for mileages over 4000;

* the flat rate allowance has been increased by 2p a mile;

* an extra band, for cars over 2000cc, has been added to the alternative scale linked to engine size.

The new rates from April 6, 1990 are:

(a) flat rate allowance for all engine sizes

Tax-free allowance
(pence per mile)

Up to 4000 miles: 32
Over 4000 miles   12.5

(b) alternative scale, based on engine size

	Tax-free allowance (pence per mile)	
	Up to 4000	*Over 4000*
Engine size (cc)	*miles*	*miles*
Up to 1000	24.5	9.5
1001 – 1500	30.0	11.5
1501 – 2000	34.0	13.5
Over 2000	43.0	16.5

It is recognised that some employees will pay more tax as a result of the changes.

Mileage allowances Sch. 4

Employees for whom the new non-statutory rules would mean a higher tax bill will see the increases introduced gradually by means of transitional arrangements.

1989/90 will be used as a base year, and the amount taxable in subsequent years will depend on whether the allowance paid in 1989/90 contained a taxable element. For an individual whose mileage allowance was within the Revenue's old rules, there will be no charge in 1990/91, and in subsequent years the ceiling on the taxable 'mileage profit' will increase by £1,000 each year.

If the 1989/90 mileage allowances exceeded the Revenue-approved amount and thus included a taxable element, the rules are more complicated. The upper limit on the taxable amount is calculated in two stages. If the business mileage in the year is greater than in 1989/90, the 1989/90 base amount is increased proportionately. A further amount is then added, starting with nil in 1990/91, £1,000 in 1991/92 and increasing by £1,000 for each subsequent year.

Capital allowances S. 87

From 1990/91 onwards, an employee who uses his own car (strictly, a mechanically propelled road vehicle, which could include other forms of transport) on his employer's business will be able to claim capital allowances on the same basis as a self-employed person who uses a car partly for business and partly for private purposes. This relief was not previously available to employees unless they could satisfy the Inspector that it was necessary for them to use a car in the performance of their duties.

The capital allowances calculations follow the normal rules, and the main points are that:

(a) if the car cost more than £8,000, the normal 25% writing down allowance is limited to £2,000 a year;

(b) the allowance is then further restricted to the business use proportion; *and*

(c) in the year of sale, a balancing allowance can be claimed if the sale price is less than the written-down value, restricted as before to the business use proportion of the difference. It would be unusual for the sale price of a car to exceed its written-down value, but if it did, part of the allowances given would be clawed back in a balancing charge.

The cost of the car will usually be the amount actually spent, but where the car was bought before it was reasonably anticipated that it would be used for business, the cost is taken as the market value at the time it was put to such use. Where the car was in use for the employment at 5 April 1990 but no capital allowances were given, the cost is the market value at 6 April 1990.

It should be noted that the claiming of capital allowances would take an individual outside the FPCS as this is deemed to include an allowance for depreciation.

Interest relief   An employee who obtains a loan to buy an asset which he uses in his employer's business and on which capital allowances are available can also claim relief for the interest paid. Consequently, the lifting of the 'necessary' restriction for the claiming of capital allowances on cars means that relief may now be claimed for interest paid on a loan to acquire a car used in the employer's business, again limited to the business use proportion.

Under the existing rules, overdraft interest does not qualify for tax relief, nor interest which falls due and payable after 5 April following the third anniversary of the loan.

16 INCOME TAX
PRIORITY SHARE ALLOCATIONS FOR EMPLOYEES

S. 79 Directors and employees given limited priority rights of allocation in a public offer of shares where the price payable is not less than the price payable by the general public are not liable to income tax on the benefit which may arise provided that shares in the company are offered on 'similar terms' to all those entitled to participate.

The new section deals with the circumstances in which directors and employees are entitled, by reason of employment, to share allocations in two or more companies whose shares are offered for sale at the same time. When two or more such companies jointly own another company they may decide to offer priority rights in their shares to the employees of that other company. These employees may be offered fewer shares in any such company than are offered to the employees of that company. The 'similar terms' rule in the existing legislation did not permit this. Section 79 provides that the 'similar terms' rule may permit such mixed priority rights to be taken into account provided that the aggregate value of the priority shares offered to such an employee is the same as the value of the entitlement of a comparable employee of any of the companies whose shares have been offered in this way.

Section 79 has particular application to the privatisation of electricity where certain companies in the industry are jointly owned by the distribution companies and wish to give the same terms in substance to the employees of both the subsidiary and distribution sets of companies.

17 INCOME TAX
EXPENSES OF ENTERTAINERS

S. 77   This new relief for payments of fees to agents by entertainers treated as employees has been introduced in an attempt to equalise the tax treatment of entertainers under Schedules D and E. The entertainers concerned are actors, musicians, singers, dancers and theatrical artists.

The position recently adopted by the Inland Revenue is that performers who have been treated as self-employed (Schedule D) since before 6 April 1987 will continue to be so treated but that performers engaged under a standard Equity contract after 5 April 1990 who had not been treated as self- employed at 5 April 1987 will be considered to be employees (Schedule E).

The rules relating to deduction of expenses under Schedule E are far more rigid than those under Schedule D as in addition to being incurred wholly and exclusively for the purposes of the profession the expense must also have been necessarily incurred. Many expenses are incurred wholly and exclusively for the purposes of a profession which are not strictly necessary for the performance of the duties. Hence, newcomers to the profession could be seen to be subjected to a more onerous tax position compared to the more established entertainer.

The problem was how to equalise the tax treatment of entertainers under Schedule D and E without creating wider ramifications for all employees. For example, the question of giving relief for travelling expenses was debated but it was considered that this would also benefit a large number of employees other than entertainers.

It has been concluded that relief for payment of fees (including VAT) to agents should be given as entertainers are unusual in having an obligation to pay agents as, in general, employment agencies are prohibited from charging fees to people looking for work.

The deduction is allowable if:

- the payment is incurred by the employee under a contract with an agent and the agent holds a current licence under the Employment Agencies Act 1973;

- the fees are calculated as a percentage of and are paid out of the employment earnings in the current tax year.

The maximum allowable deduction is 17.5% of the emoluments of the employment in the relevant tax year.

The method of giving relief is currently under consideration with a proposal for relief to be given at source by the employer: ie agent's fees (up to 17.5%) would be deducted from gross pay and PAYE operated on the balance. In the meantime, claims to relief should be made to the entertainer's tax office after the end of the tax year, although the tax office may agree to give some provisional relief by adjusting the entertainer's current PAYE code number.

18 INCOME TAX
TRANSFERS OF ASSETS ABROAD

S.66   The provisions which prevent the transfer by individuals ordinarily resident in the UK of income earning assets outside of the UK tax net (S.739 to S.746 TA) are refined such that assets transferred to a company incorporated and hence resident in the UK under domestic law, but deemed not resident under a double tax treaty, are brought within the provisions. The information powers under those sections are also similarly extended. These changes are effective from 20 March 1990.

19 INCOME TAX TAXES MANAGEMENT ACT

Returns
S. 90

The Revenue are to be given greater flexibility over the design and content of income tax return forms.

From 6 April 1990, a notice issued by an Inspector (normally printed on the tax return form) can require the person to whom it is addressed to provide such information, accounts and statements, for any period or periods, as is considered necessary by the Inspector for the purposes of assessing the person to income tax or capital gains tax (new S.8 TMA and S.12 TMA). The requirement that every return shall include a declaration, by the person making it, that it is to the best of his knowledge correct and complete, remains.

A similar change is made in relation to trustee and partnership returns.

There is no longer a statutory requirement that the return show income and capital gains computed in accordance with the Taxes Acts or that each separate source should be specified. However there is little doubt that notices and tax return forms issued in future will require such information. The requirements of the notice by the Inspector will now have statutory effect, provided they are for the purposes of assessment of tax.

Revenue
information
powers
Ss. 93 & 125

The Revenue are now given powers to obtain information required by foreign fiscal authorities. Details are contained in *36: Information and returns*, as are provisions relating to notices requiring persons to deliver documents to the Revenue.

S. 72   The annual exempt amount for capital gains tax remains at £5,000 and the rate remains dependent on the income tax rate of the taxpayer.

However, with the advent of independent taxation, both husband and wife will each be entitled to the annual exemption from 6 April 1990.

21 EMPLOYEE SHARE OWNERSHIP TRUSTS (ESOPs)

In order to encourage companies wishing to promote employee share ownership, FA 1989 introduced statutory tax deductions for payments by a company to a qualifying employee share ownership trust (QUEST) set up to acquire and distribute shares to its employees. Numerous conditions must be met in order to qualify.

The relief is in addition to that which may be available under general tax principles, i.e. for revenue expenditure laid out wholly and exclusively for the purposes of a trade. This followed the 1972 tax case of Heather v P-E Consulting Group Ltd. Partly for this reason, but also because of the restrictive nature of the conditions in FA 1989, few (if any) employers have so far found it worthwhile to set up a QUEST, although some have established similar arrangements on a non-approved basis.

Ss. 31-40 An attempt to make the QUEST more attractive is made by enabling a form of roll-over relief to be claimed by existing shareholders in the founding company who realise capital gains on sales of their shares to the QUEST trustees. The relief will be available to shareholders of both public and private companies but will be of greater interest to the latter. There are complex and detailed conditions which must be satisfied before this relief will be given.

Availability of relief S.31 The following seven conditions must all be satisfied:

1. A disposal of shares is made by the claimant to the trustees of a QUEST which was established by a company which immediately after the disposal was a trading company or the holding company of a trading group.

2. The shares must be non-redeemable, fully paid-up ordinary shares in the founding company. There must be no restrictions attaching to the shares other than restrictions attaching to all shares of the same class, or restrictions imposed by the founding company's articles of association, requiring disposal of shares on ceasing to be a director or employee.

3. Within 12 months of the date of the disposal to them the trustees must be beneficially entitled to not less than 10% of the founding company's ordinary share capital, its profits available for distribution and its assets on winding up. These tests are determined by reference to similar requirements in the group relief legislation.

4. The person making the disposal must obtain consideration for it, and, either within six months of that disposal or, if later, within six months of the date when the trustees become 10% shareholders as referred to in 3. above, he must apply all or part of that consideration in the purchase of replacement assets. Alternatively, within the same time frame, he must have entered into an unconditional contract for the acquisition of replacement assets.

Replacement
assets
Ss. 34-35

Replacement assets are widely defined to include any chargeable assets under the normal CGT rules except shares or debentures in the founding company (or in a member of the same group). However, the replacement asset (whether purchased directly or by exercise of an option) may not be a dwelling house or part of a dwelling house or land which would be eligible for exemption from capital gains tax under S.101 (1) CGTA 1979 (relief on disposal of private residence) if disposed of by the claimant or his spouse (S.34). Similarly, the replacement asset may not consist of shares which become subject to a claim for relief under the business expansion scheme (S.35).

In respect of the replacement assets, the claimant must also be within the scope of CGT (i.e. UK resident or ordinarily resident or non-resident but trading in the UK through a branch or agency) in respect of the replacement asset and must not be protected from CGT by reason of any double taxation convention.

5. Between the date of the initial disposal and the acquisition of the replacement assets, or if later the time when the trustees satisfy the 10% requirement at 3. above, neither the claimant nor any person connected with him must be able to reacquire any of the shares or rights therein other than:

- by operation of pre-emption provisions in the circumstances described in 2. above, *or*

- by reason of being a beneficiary under the trust, *or*

- through appropriation under an approved profit-sharing scheme.

6. No chargeable event in relation to the trustees must occur in any year of assessment (or in any accounting period if the claimant is a company) during which the claimant makes his disposal or his acquisition of replacement assets or at any time between those two periods.

Chargeable events in relation to the QUEST trustees are defined in S.69(1) FA 1989 to include non-qualifying transfers of shares, transfers on non-qualifying terms, retention of shares for more than seven years, and expenditure for non-qualifying purposes.

7. The disposal must be made on or after 20 March 1990.

The relief
S. 33

The relief operates on a similar basis to that for replacement of business assets (S.115 CGTA).

On making a claim within two years of the date of acquisition of the replacement asset, the claimant will for CGT purposes be treated as if:

a) the consideration received for the disposal of the shares to the QUEST trustees (the QUEST shares) is of such amount as gives rise to neither a gain nor a loss; *and*

b) the cost of acquisition of the replacement asset is reduced by the gain on the disposal of the QUEST shares.

If the whole of the disposal proceeds of the QUEST shares is reinvested in acquiring the replacement asset, the base cost of the replacement asset will be the original cost of the QUEST shares plus any excess over the disposal proceeds invested in acquiring the replacement asset. There will be no CGT charge on the disposal to the QUEST.

Example

QUEST shares − original cost	£7
− disposal proceeds	£11
Replacement asset − cost	£16
Gain on disposal of QUEST shares	NIL
Base cost of replacement asset	£12

If only part of the QUEST disposal proceeds is reinvested in a replacement asset but the amount not reinvested is less than the gain on the QUEST share disposal, partial relief will be available. The amount not reinvested will be subject to CGT and the base cost of the replacement asset will be treated as reduced to the original acquisition cost of the QUEST shares.

Example

QUEST shares − original cost	£7
− disposal proceeds	£11
Replacement asset − cost	£8
Gain on disposal of QUEST shares	£3
Base cost of replacement asset	£7

If the amount reinvested in the replacement asset is less than the original acquisition cost of the QUEST shares, no roll-over relief will be available as the whole of the gain on the QUEST shares will be treated as having been realised.

Example

QUEST shares − original cost	£7
− disposal proceeds	£11
Replacement asset − cost	£6
Gain on disposal of QUEST shares	£4
Base cost of replacement asset	£6

The granting of roll-over relief to the claimant will not affect the CGT position of the QUEST trustees nor the vendor of the replacement asset.

The normal CGT rules for determining the amount of the consideration deemed to be given for a disposal or acquisition are to be applied before the roll-over provisions (e.g. where the parties are not at arms length the consideration will be deemed to be the open market value).

Subsequent *chargeable* *event* *S.36*

If roll-over relief is claimed and, while the claimant or a connected person still owns all or any of the replacement asset, a chargeable event occurs in relation to the QUEST trustees, a claw-back of the relief will take place whereby the claimant will be deemed to have sold the replacement assets and reacquired them at such value as secures that the rolled over QUEST gain becomes chargeable to CGT at that time.

However, if before a chargeable event occurs 'anything has happened as regards any of the replacement assets such that it can be said that a charge has accrued in respect of any of the gain rolled over', then on the happening of the chargeable event the amount chargeable to CGT will be adjusted and reduced in a manner which is 'just and reasonable'. It is difficult to envisage the criteria to be used in applying this subsection.

It still seems possible to transfer the assets into trust without crystallising a CGT charge (i.e. subject to hold over relief being available under S.147A or S.126 CGTA), and this may determine whether tax arises on a later chargeable event. If the trustees are *not* the persons 'beneficially entitled' to the assets and the beneficiaries are not connected with the settlor, no claw-back charge would arise even though the trustees are connected with the settlor. Where the beneficiaries are so connected they may be subject to the claw-back charge although it is the trustees who actually own the assets.

S.37

Provisions similar to those in Section 36 deal with the position where the replacement assets have been the subject of a disposal and the proceeds have been reinvested in business assets with the benefit of roll-over relief under Sections 115-121 CGTA. In such circumstances the gain previously rolled over under Section 33 will crystallise on the occurrence of the chargeable event on the same basis as outlined in Section 36.

S.38

This provision deals with the situation where the replacement assets were shares which have been substituted by qualifying corporate bonds on a reorganisation, conversion, reconstruction, etc within Schedule 13 FA 1984.

The charge arising on the occurrence of a 'chargeable event' is imposed in broadly the same manner as under Section 36. However, the gain which crystallises will be the lesser of the gain rolled over under Section 33 and the deemed gain which would arise under Para 10(1)(b) Sch 13 FA 1984 if it were to apply at the date of the chargeable event. The latter provision brings into charge the gain which arose but was deferred when the reorganisation, etc occurred, limiting the S.67 CGTA exemption for gains on qualifying corporate bonds only to appreciation accruing after the reorganisation, etc. Where the Schedule 13 deemed disposal gives rise to an allowable loss, no claw-back occurs but there is no allowable loss.

Information
S.39
The trustees of a QUEST can be required to make a return of shares sold to them on which a roll over claim has been made. The return may require the trustees to provide information which the inspector needs for the purposes of a claw-back including information on expenditure incurred by the trustees, and assets acquired and transferred by them. Penalties under S.98 TMA are chargeable if the necessary return is not made.

Where a roll-over relief claim has been made, the inspector will send a certificate to the trustees confirming that the relief has been allowed.

S.40
Section 40 makes amendments to other enactments consequential on the new QUEST provisions.

22 | LOANS TO TRADERS

S. 83 Relief is available under Section 136 CGTA to persons who have made qualifying loans to UK traders or payments under guarantee of such loans where the whole or part of those loans become irrecoverable. A capital gain is deemed to arise in certain circumstances where all or part of the loan is later recovered.

Amendments are now introduced to ensure that the following amounts subsequently recovered on or after 20 March 1990 (and not already treated as gains) are so chargeable:

a) recoveries of payments made under a guarantee of the principal of the loan or of interest in respect of the loan;

b) recoveries by one company of amounts loaned by another company in the same Section 272 TA 70 group. For this purpose, two companies are in the same group if they were in the same group when the loan was made or have been in the same group at any subsequent time;

c) recoveries by one company of payments under any guarantee of principal or interest made by another company in the same Section 272 TA 70 group; *and*

d) recoveries by one company of principal or interest on a loan in respect of which another company in the same Section 272 TA 70 group has made any payment under guarantee.

23 | DEEP GAIN SECURITIES – INTRODUCTION

FA 1989 introduced a new system for taxing 'deep gain securities' i.e. securities issued at a discount of more than ½ % per annum or more than 15 % overall and which contain at least one variable feature, such as an indexed coupon or variable redemption proceeds. Disposals of deep gain securities after 14 March 1989 give rise to a charge under Case III or Case IV of Schedule D on the whole of the difference between the cost of acquisition and the disposal or redemption proceeds.

The deep gain provisions applied, inter alia, to most bonds convertible into share capital of the issuing company where, on exercise of an option by the issuer or the investor, the bond was repaid before maturity at a premium, and to bonds linked to an index of equity values. During the course of the 1989 Bill it was announced that:

a) the deep gain provisions would be narrowed so that a bond would not be caught simply because of its option provisions;

b) certain convertible and index linked bonds issued before 9 June 1989 would be excluded; *and*

c) consultations would take place as to the tax treatment of future issues of such securities.

These changes which were announced last year but were not included as amendments to the 1989 provisions are now contained in the 1990 Act as explained in the following three sections.

Section 56, the shortest section, introduces Schedule 10 – the longest and, arguably, the most complex of the 1990 schedules. The Financial Secretary, during the course of the Standing Committee debate, acknowledged the labyrinthine nature of the Schedule but attributed this to the range and complexity of the convertible securities whose tax treatment it seeks to address. The aim is to allow the City to retain its leading position in designing and adapting such instruments for a wide range of customers while closing any tax avoidance loopholes. The legislation was foreshadowed by the consultative document entitled *'Tax treatment of convertible and equity indexed securities'* which was issued by the Inland Revenue in October 1989. Several bodies made representations in response to this document and the legislation purports to take account of these representations and consultations with the market.

In essence, Schedule 10 introduces a new concept, 'qualifying convertible securities', and lays down rules for taxing the holders of such securities and, in certain circumstances, allowing relief to issuing companies.

S. 56 &
Sch. 10

The new rules apply where a 'qualifying convertible security' is

a) transferred by way of sale, exchange or gift on or after 9 June 1989 and is subject to at least one 'qualifying provision for redemption' (as defined below) under which the occasion for redemption has not arisen; *or*

b) redeemed by the holder on or after 9 June 1989 by exercise of an option for redemption under a 'qualifying provision for redemption' to which the security is subject.

A 'qualifying convertible security' is one which satisfies the following conditions:

a) it was issued by a company on or after 9 June 1989;

b) it is not a share in the company, it is redeemable and it was not issued in circumstances such that it was a distribution of a company;

c) at the time of issue it was quoted on the official list of a recognised stock exchange;

d) under the terms of issue:

- it is convertible into ordinary shares of the issuer

- it either carries no right to interest or the interest rate is fixed and determined at the time of issue, *and*

- the amount due on redemption and any interest is payable in the currency in which the issue price is denominated;

e) at the time of issue there is only one qualifying provision for redemption;

f) the yield to redemption is no more than a reasonable commercial return;

g) the security in question is either a deep gain or deep discount security only because of a qualifying provision for redemption;

h) obtaining a tax advantage was not the main benefit or one of the main benefits which were expected to accrue from the issue;

i) where interest is payable it falls due at regular six-month or annual periods.

A 'qualifying provision for redemption' exists in relation to a security where:

a) redemption before maturity is only at the option of the holder;

b) such redemption is provided for on one occasion only;

c) redemption is to occur on the last day of an income period (i.e. the due date for interest where interest is payable, or annually from the date of issue where no interest is payable);

d) the amount payable on exercising the option to redeem is fixed, is determined at the time the security becomes subject to the provision, and constitutes a deep gain.

A qualifying convertible security is taken outside the ambit of the deep gain legislation for so long as it meets the qualifying conditions. A holder of a qualifying convertible security who sells it before the expiry of his put option (including a further option acquired after issue) or exercises the option to put the security back to the issuer will not be subject to the rigours of the deep gain rules but, instead, will be subject to tax under Case III or Case IV of Schedule D in respect of the 'total income element' during his period of ownership and to CGT for any residual gain.

The 'total income element' is, in essence, that part of the yield to redemption during the period of ownership of the security which is not represented by interest paid.

Provision is made for the new system to apply to securities held in the premiums trust funds of Lloyd's underwriters.

Where a qualifying convertible security is redeemed on or after 9 June 1989 in circumstances such that the new rules apply to the holder, the issuing company will be entitled to a deduction against its profits for the accounting period in which the redemption occurs in respect of the excess of the amount paid on redemption over the issue price of the security.

An investor who sells a security after all put options have expired will normally be subject only to CGT.

An investor who converts a security into shares will normally be liable only to CGT with the charge being rolled over into the shares.

25 | INDEXED SECURITIES

S.58   'Qualifying indexed securities' as defined in FA 1989 Schedule 11 Para 2 are taken out of the deep gains rules. Section 58 expands the meaning of qualifying indexed securities to include securities linked to a published share index and issued before 9 June 1989 which, although not themselves quoted at the time of issue, are quoted on a recognised stock exchange on 8 June 1989 and such securities issued on or after 9 June 1989 which obtain a listing within one month of issue.

Provision is also made for securities where the amount payable on redemption is a minimum amount of 10% or less of the issue price to be capable of being qualifying indexed securities; the figure of 10% is wholly arbitrary and is designed simply to ensure that the bond has a floor value and thus constitutes a debt. Similarly, securities issued on or after 9 June 1989 will be capable of being qualifying indexed securities even though the terms of issue provide for redemption at not more than the issue price where the issuing company is taken over, the issuer fails to comply with his duties, and in certain other external circumstances.

26 | OTHER EXCLUSIONS

Ss.57 & 59
& Sch.10

One of the hallmarks of a deep gain security is that the amount payable on redemption might constitute a deep gain. Section 57 provides that, for this purpose, redemption does not include redemption before maturity where the issuer fails to comply with the duties imposed by the terms of issue, becomes unable to pay his debts or, where the issuer is a company, a person gains control by way of an offer to acquire shares.

Other consequential exclusions from the definitions of a deep discount security are necessary. Firstly, a security issued on or after 1 August 1990 will not be a deep discount security if the terms of issue provide for more than one date on which the holder may require redemption. Other exclusions are:

a) a security issued by a company on or after 1 August 1990 which is convertible into share capital in a company (whether or not the issuer)

b) a qualifying convertible security (as defined above).

QUALIFYING CORPORATE BONDS

Qualifying corporate bonds are exempt from CGT and this has meant that capital losses cannot be established. On the other hand, those making loans to traders which are not corporate bonds are able in certain circumstances to obtain relief for a capital loss if part or all of the loan is irrecoverable. In order to rectify this anomaly, qualifying corporate bonds are brought into the scheme of relief for loans to traders in Section 136 CGTA.

A qualifying corporate bond will rank for relief if it is issued after 14 March 1989 (or, if issued before then, was held on 15 March 1989 by the original investor) and it meets the conditions of Section 136 CGTA, i.e. the money lent is used by a UK resident borrower for the purposes of a trade carried on by him, etc.

If, on a claim by the investor, the inspector is satisfied that certain conditions are met, a capital loss will be allowed. Relief is due in the following circumstances:

a) the value of the security has become negligible, the claimant has not assigned his right to recover any part of the principal and the claimant and the borrower have not been members of the same group of companies during the life of the loan; *or*

b) the security's redemption date has passed, all of the outstanding principal is irrecoverable and the assignment and group relationship tests in *a)* are satisfied; *or*

c) the security's redemption date has passed, part of the outstanding principal is irrecoverable and the assignment and group relationship tests in *a)* are satisfied.

The amount of relief due for a security within *a)* or *b)* is the lesser of the outstanding principal and the cost of acquisition of the security. For a security within *c)* the relief due is the difference between the cost of acquisition and the amount of any principal which has been recovered plus any amount which, in the inspector's opinion, is recoverable.

Where relief for a capital loss has been allowed and the claimant later recovers all or part of the outstanding principal the recovery will constitute a chargeable gain.

Reorganisations, etc
S.85

This section amplifies provisions on corporate reorganisations involving qualifying corporate bonds (in FA 1984 Schedule 13) to take account of the Section 84 provisions. The effect is that where an allowable loss has arisen (other than on an actual disposal) under Section 84 in respect of a bond which was acquired as consideration for chargeable shares or securities on a corporate reorganisation conversion, reconstruction, etc, a later disposal of the bond is to be treated as occurring at the same time as relief for the Section 84 loss was allowed.

28 | RATES OF CORPORATION TAX

S.19   The rate of corporation tax for the financial year commencing 1 April 1990 remains unchanged at 35%.

Small companies'   The rate of corporation tax chargeable on small companies (other than close
rate   investment companies — CICs) for the financial year 1990 is 25%. CICs are
S.20   not eligible for the small companies' rate.

A non-CIC may claim the benefit of the small companies' rate if its profits do not exceed £200,000 (financial year 1989 - £150,000). Where a company's profits exceed £200,000 but are less than £1,000,000 (financial year 1989 - £750,000), the corporation tax charged on its basic profits may be reduced by a fraction being 1/40 of the difference between £1,000,000 and the company's profits. These upper and lower limits are reduced proportionately for accounting periods of less than 12 months and, where there are active associated companies, are divided by one plus the number of active associated companies which the company has in the accounting period.

Where a company's accounting period spans 1 April 1990 the company's profits are apportioned between the period to 31 March 1990 and the period from 1 April 1990 for the purpose of applying the above limits.

29 | CONTRIBUTIONS TO LEAs, TECs AND LECs

S. 75   Contributions by businesses to approved local enterprise agencies (LEAs) are specifically deductible for tax purposes from the profits or gains of those businesses (S.79 TA). This requires that to qualify as tax deductions such contributions should confer no benefit on the person making the contribution (or on any connected person) and must be made on or after 1 April 1982 and before 1 April 1992. Section 75 extends this period to 1 April 1995.

S. 76   Contributions made by businesses to training and enterprise councils (TECs) or local enterprise companies (LECs) on or after 1 April 1990 and before 1 April 1995 will now be given the same tax deductible status as contributions to approved LEAs. Again, no benefit should be conferred on the person making the contribution (or on any connected person).

LEAs provide advice on starting small businesses. TECs are private sector bodies which are responsible for the Government's training and enterprise programmes in their areas. With boards consisting mainly of local business people, they will work under contract to the Department of Employment's Training Agency. LECs fulfil the same function in Scotland.

30
CORPORATION TAX
COMPANY GIFTS

Ss. 26, 27 & 94 The single gift relief for companies introduced by FA 1986 has been extended to bring it into line with the £600 minimum and £5 million maximum limits for individuals (see *9: Charitable giving*). Companies will be able to obtain relief against their profits chargeable to corporation tax for gifts of money which, after deduction of basic rate tax, do not exceed £5 million so, at the current basic rate of 25%, the maximum gift on which relief is available will be £6,666,667. Companies (other than close companies) can currently obtain relief for gifts up to the equivalent of 3% of dividends paid in the accounting period on their ordinary share capital, and this will remain the upper limit if it is more favourable than the new provisions. Companies which are themselves charities are, however, unable to benefit from the new provisions.

Close companies, as defined by S.414 TA 1988 (broadly those which are controlled by five or fewer persons) were unable to benefit from the FA 1986 relief, but are within the scope of the new provisions. However, they are subject to restrictions not applicable to other companies, similar to those for gifts by individuals. The gift must have no condition for repayment, provide no benefit to the company nor any connected person or company, nor be part of an arrangement involving the acquisition of property by the charity from the company or connected person otherwise than by way of gift. Close companies are also unable to make use of the dividend-related upper limit for relief.

S. 27 The maximum relief is shared among companies associated with one another at any time during the accounting period, but companies which are themselves charities or which are dormant are disregarded in determining the number of associated companies. A company is associated with another if one has control of the other, or both are under the control of the same person or persons.

The relief available to each company is determined by dividing the £5 million net maximum by one plus the number of associated companies. Thus if a company has 99 associates, the maximum gift it can make which will qualify for relief is £50,000 (net). Inland Revenue Technical Division has confirmed that there is no exclusion for non-resident companies and, despite tabled Opposition amendments, no relaxation has been given for companies in multinational groups. No account is taken of associated companies, however, where the alternative dividend-related upper limit for relief applies.

For accounting periods of less than twelve months, the maximum relief is reduced proportionally.

As for all other tax-effective charitable gifts, basic rate tax must be deducted at source and paid over to the Revenue. The charity then claims repayment of the tax deducted, and the company obtains relief for the gross payment as a charge on income deductible from its profits charged to corporation tax. The company must give to the charity a certificate stating that basic rate tax has been deducted, and that the gift meets the additional tests for a close company.

The new provisions apply to gifts made on or after 1 October 1990.

S. 94   Powers are given to the Board to require the charity to produce for inspection all books, documents, etc containing information relating to gifts in respect of which the charity has claimed repayment, and penalties can be imposed for failure to comply.

31 CORPORATION TAX
DEFINITION OF A GROUP

S. 86 The definition of a group for capital gains tax purposes (S.272 TA 70) required from 14 March 1989 that, inter alia, the equity holders, as defined, are entitled to at least 50% of the profits and of the assets on a winding up. If arrangements existed for such entitlement to be reduced below 50% in a subsequent period it would previously have prevented that subsidiary from being a member of the group.

Section 86 provides that a company will fail to be part of the group, under this part of the test, only if the actual entitlement of the equity holders is less than 50% at the relevant time.

The principal company in the group can, however, elect for the old provisions to apply until 25 January 1990, and has two years from the end of its first accounting period ending after 31 January 1990 in which to do so.

32 | CORPORATION TAX
DUAL-RESIDENT COMPANIES

Capital gains
S.65

Various provisions which allow capital gains tax liabilities to be deferred are deemed not to apply if the acquiring company, although resident in the UK under domestic law, would be non-UK resident by virtue of a double tax treaty and would be protected from any UK tax on a subsequent disposal of the asset under the provisions of the relevant treaty.

The reliefs which no longer apply are: intra-group transfers on a no gain no loss basis under Section 273 TA 70; transfers on a no gain no loss basis under the company reconstruction provisions in Section 267 TA 70; and roll-over relief within a group of companies under Section 276 TA 70. The new rules operate for transfers from 20 March 1990 except with respect to roll-over relief where relief will still be available if the acquisition took place before that date and the disposal takes place within a year of the acquisition (or such longer period as the Board may determine).

Transfer of
assets abroad
S.66

Similar rules are introduced with respect to the transfer by ordinarily resident individuals of assets outside the UK tax net. For further details, see *18: Transfers of assets abroad.*

Controlled foreign
companies
S.67

Under anti-avoidance provisions designed to prevent profits being accumulated in offshore tax havens, profits of controlled foreign companies (CFC) can be attributed back to the controlling UK shareholders.

From 20 March 1990 profits of a company which is UK resident under domestic legislation but resident elsewhere under the terms of a double tax treaty will be within the ambit of the CFC rules. Further, the acceptable distribution policy, which can prevent any attribution of profits back to the UK controlling shareholders, will not be effective unless the dividend is brought into charge in the hands of the UK shareholders. Thus, if under domestic law the subsidiary is UK resident, any dividend paid up within a UK group would not be subject to tax in the hands of the shareholder, and the test could not, therefore, be met.

33 EC CAPITAL MOVEMENTS

S. 68 Section 765(1) TA makes unlawful, without Treasury consent, the following capital transactions:

1. where a UK resident company causes or permits a non-UK resident company which it controls to create or issue any shares or debentures; *and*

2. where a UK resident company transfers (or causes or permits to be transferred) to any person any shares or debentures of a non-UK resident company which it controls, except for the purpose of enabling a person to act as a director.

General consents are, however, available in a number of different circumstances.

Section 68 of the Finance Act removes the requirement for Treasury consent for the above transactions carried out on or after 1 July 1990 which involve movements of capital between member states of the EC. Instead, the Section imposes a requirement to provide details of the transactions to the Board.

Movements of capital are defined by reference to Article 1 of the Directive of the Council of the EC of 24 June 1988 No 88/361/EEC, which is an all-embracing definition covering all types of capital investment.

There will be no requirement to give details of those transactions covered by the general consents before 1 July 1990.

Section 98 TMA is consequentially amended to include penalties for failure to comply with this new requirement. The maximum penalty is £3,000 plus £600 for each day after the imposition of the penalty on which the failure continues.

34 | EUROPEAN ECONOMIC INTEREST GROUPINGS (EEIGs)

S.69 & Sch.11   From 1 July 1989, European Economic Interest Groupings (EEIGs) are to be chargeable to tax on the basis of grouping members being regarded as owning a share of any assets and being taxed as a partnership in respect of any trading activities. However, assessments are not to be raised by reference to the profits of the grouping as a whole, as is the case for partnerships of individuals, but by reference to the profit share of the individual members. Each assessment will be made on the grouping as agent for the individual members.

A member's share of any assets is determined in accordance with the contract setting up the group or, if the contract is silent on this, in accordance with profit sharing ratios or, if profit sharing is not stipulated, equally among the members.

Members are treated as acquiring or disposing of a share in an asset not only when the group disposes of or acquires assets, but also when there is a change in the members of the grouping.

There are no specific provisions to protect members from a charge to tax when there is a change in membership interests, but it is understood that where the grouping trades the Revenue will apply the concession that applies to partnerships. The position in non-trading situations is less clear. This may be particularly important if relevant treaty protection is not available.

An inspector is given authority by notice to require in relation to a grouping a return of such information and supporting documents as are specified in the notice. In the case of EEIGs registered in Great Britain or Northern Ireland the notice should be served on the EEIG itself. In the case of other EEIGs the notice should be given to any UK resident member of the EEIG or, if none exist, to any member of the EEIG. Every return must include a declaration by the person making it that the return is correct and complete (to the best of the maker's knowledge).

In complying with the requirements of a notice under these provisions an EEIG acts through any of its managers. Where the managers of an EEIG do not include an individual the EEIG is required to act through the designated representative of any of the managers. The declaration on any return must be made by the appropriate number of managers where an EEIG's contract of formation provides that it shall be validly bound only by two or more managers acting jointly.

Schedule 11 also amends TMA to include a penalty for failure to comply with a notice under these provisions. The EEIG or member on whom the notice is served will be liable to a maximum penalty of £300 plus £60 for each day after the imposition of the penalty on which the failure continues. Where an incorrect return is made fraudulently or negligently by an EEIG or any of its members the maximum penalty shall be £3,000 multiplied by the number of members of the EEIG at the time the return is made.

35 | TRANSFER OF A UK BRANCH OR AGENCY

S. 70 From 20 March 1990, it is possible to incorporate a UK branch or agency of a non-resident company without suffering potentially penal tax consequences. Previously, although relief existed with respect to the transfer of losses and avoidance of capital allowance recaptures, such a transaction could have given a potential capital gains tax charge on the value of chargeable assets transferred, including any goodwill of the business.

From 20 March, provided a trade or part of a trade is being transferred to a UK resident group company a relief akin to that provided for intra-group transfers under Section 273 TA 70 will be available. Similarly, any charge arising from assets ceasing to be used for a UK trade (under Section 127(3) FA 89) is overridden. The definition of group for these purposes is the same as for Section 272 TA 70 but without the requirement that all members of the group must be UK resident.

The relief will not, however, be available if the transferee is:

- a dual-resident investing company within Section 404 TA;

- a company which would be treated as resident outside the UK under the provisions of any treaty such that a gain on the disposal of the assets would not be subject to UK tax; *or*

- an investment trust.

The relief is also not available in circumstances where a disposal by the non-resident company of any branch asset would not be within the charge to UK tax. It is not clear what this provision is designed to achieve.

For the relief to be available a claim must be made by both companies within two years of the end of the accounting period of the transferee in which the transfer took place.

If the transferee is subsequently sold outside of the worldwide group there is no deemed disposal and reacquisition by the transferee under Section 278 TA 70.

Revenue information powers S.125

Section 20 TMA enables the Revenue to call for documents in the possession or power of the taxpayer or other persons, or to call for particulars to be furnished, which are relevant to the tax liability of a taxpayer under scrutiny. Hitherto the provision has been strictly limited to UK tax exposure although in conformity with the Directive of the Council of European Communities No.77/799/EEC on mutual assistance the Revenue have been required to supply information obtained in connection with a taxpayer's affairs to tax authorities of other EC member States.

The new provision extends the Revenue powers further by substituting, for references to UK tax and legislation in Sections 20 and 20B TMA, references to taxes on income and capital under any provision of the law of other member States and references to the provision in accordance with which the foreign tax is charged. Accordingly, even where the Revenue do not require the information sought in connection with UK tax exposure, they will, under Section 125, nevertheless have the same authority to obtain information on behalf of the foreign fiscal authority. This will, in effect, place the Revenue in the position of an agent of that authority in foreign tax investigation matters.

The provision relates not only to an exchange of information already obtained in relation to a UK liability, but also to information sought expressly for the purposes of the potential foreign liability. Accordingly there must be some conjecture as to how the provision will work in practice. Whilst the foreign fiscal authority will no doubt liaise with the Revenue on what is required to be obtained, the ability of a taxpayer in the UK legitimately to resist surrender of documents and information not relevant to the foreign liability will be dependent on ease of access to his foreign adviser. However, it is to be hoped that a reasonable period of time will be given to the taxpayer to furnish the information in question prior to the issue of the notice. Furthermore, it may be that drafting inadequacies provide the taxpayer with an unexpected loophole. One leading commentator has already pointed out that the lack of certain appropriate consequential legislative amendments necessitated by the extension of the Revenue powers into the international arena may well severely restrict the intended scope of the provisions.

Similar provisions have been introduced in respect of inheritance tax. For further details see *49: Inheritance tax*.

Returns under
pay and file
S. 91

When the system of 'pay and file' for assessing and collecting corporation tax begins (which is not expected to be before 1993), companies will be required to provide information, accounts, statements and reports. The information which may be requested is that which is relevant to the corporation tax affairs of the company and during debates on the Bill it was made clear that the reports to which the section refers are mainly — but not exclusively — those required by the Companies Act 1989, e.g. the directors' and auditors' reports. From 26 July 1990, statutory effect is also given to the present wording of the return form that it is correct and complete 'to the best of the knowledge' of the person completing it.

Provision is also made for a simplified return to be used for making amendments to the main pay and file return.

Restrictions on
Board's power to
call for
information
S. 93

Section 20(2) TMA empowers the Board to require a person to deliver documents, etc containing information relevant to his tax liability. Section 93 restricts this power to cases where the Board have reasonable grounds to believe that the person in question has failed or may fail to comply with his obligations and that such failure may seriously prejudice proper assessment or collection of tax.

37 | DETERMINATIONS UNDER PAY AND FILE

Determination procedure S. 95

When the pay and file system is introduced an inspector will be given power to determine the amount of a company's trading losses and capital allowances, management expenses and charges on income available for surrender as group relief where he is satisfied with the return. If he is not satisfied with the return, or a return has not been made, an inspector may determine the amount to the best of his judgement. An attempt was made during the passage of the Bill to widen the determination procedures to cover capital losses, surplus franked investment income and surplus ACT carried forward but the relevant amendment was withdrawn when the Economic Secretary stated that, on balance, it was better to continue the present practice of informally agreeing amounts carried forward leaving unagreed amounts to be 'hammered out' if and when they become material for tax purposes.

Appeals to the General or Special Commissioners may be made against determinations in the same manner as appeals against assessments to tax.

Where an inspector discovers that an amount determined was excessive he may issue a direction that the original determination is to be reduced by a specified amount. Such a direction may be appealed against.

The time limit for a determination of a loss, etc is six years from the end of the relevant accounting period. A direction in relation to an earlier determination may be made not later than six years from the end of the accounting period to which the determination referred, except where the excess relief arose through fraud or negligence in which case the time limit is 20 years.

Group relief amendments S. 96

Where, under pay and file and following a formal determination by the inspector, an amount surrendered as group relief is excessive (because, for example, the surrendering company has been allowed relief in its own assessment) the surrendering company must reduce or withdraw its surrender consent within 30 days of the determination. Where this has not been done the inspector, or the surrendering company if it so claims, may specify how the adjustment is to be made.

Tax to which a company is liable because of a reduction or withdrawal of group relief which is unpaid after six months may be recovered from any other company which has benefited from group relief surrendered for the accounting period by the same surrendering company.

See *38: Claims under pay and file* for a description of the general group relief provisions under pay and file.

38
TAXES MANAGEMENT – CORPORATE
CLAIMS UNDER PAY AND FILE

Payment of tax credits S.97

Under pay and file a company may claim repayment of a tax credit in making its return of profits.

Repayment of income tax S.98

Similarly, a company may claim repayment of income tax deducted at source in making its return of profits. Moreover, the bar on claims to repayment of income tax until final determination of the relevant corporation tax liability will be removed. This means that interim repayments may be claimed as of right where the income tax suffered exceeds corporation tax not in dispute.

Loss relief S.99

From the inception of pay and file it will no longer be necessary for a company to make a formal claim to carry forward trading losses against trading profits of a later year.

Claims will still have to be made to set off trading losses against non-trade profits.

Similarly, in relation to Case VI Schedule D losses no formal carry-forward claim will be necessary.

Group relief Ss.100,101 & Sch.15

New rules are introduced for the making of group relief claims which will come into effect when the pay and file system begins. The general intention is that groups of companies should not be disadvantaged, so far as group relief claims are concerned, when pay and file comes into force so that they continue to enjoy the advantages of the present fairly flexible regime. The Bill, as originally drafted, allowed a company to reallocate a trading loss which had been carried forward under the provisions of Section 393(1) TA so as to allow that loss to be surrendered as group relief; however, the reallocation had to be made within two years of the end of the accounting period of claim. After representations had been made this rather restrictive time limit was withdrawn and effectively replaced with the time limit for making group relief claims in general which is the earliest of:

a) two years from the end of the claimant's accounting period where the corporation tax assessment on the claimant has become final and conclusive;

b) the date the relevant assessment becomes final and conclusive if later than two years from the end of the accounting period;

c) six years from the end of the accounting period; *and*

d) six years and three months where an assessment has been made for an accounting period and it is under appeal.

The Board has discretion to extend the two- and six-year time limits but has indicated that this will only be exercised where the time limit was missed for reasons beyond the company's control.

A claim to group relief, which should be accompanied by a copy of the notice of consent to surrender, is to be included in the return of the claimant company's profits or by amendment to the return. The notice of surrender will have to contain details of the claimant and of the amount surrendered. This will impose greater requirements than are currently indicated by the case of Gallic Leasing Ltd v Coburn.

Where a surrender consent relates to a loss in respect of which relief has been given under Section 393(1), the surrendering company's notice of consent must be accompanied by an amended return under Section 11 TMA for the period in which relief for the brought forward loss was given. For this purpose, relief under Section 393(1) is to be treated as given for losses incurred in earlier accounting periods before those of later accounting periods.

Capital allowances
Ss.102 & 103 &
Schs. 16 & 17

New rules apply to capital allowance claims for accounting periods ending after the day from which the pay and file regime for companies is introduced.

After that date, claims for capital allowances must be made, varied or withdrawn within whichever is the shortest period of:

a) a period ending on the date when the company's corporation tax assessment for the accounting period to which the claim relates becomes final, or two years from the end of the accounting period if longer;

b) six years from the end of the accounting period to which the claim relates; *or*

c) six years and three months, where:

• the company has been assessed to corporation tax within six years of the end of the accounting period; *and*

• the assessment is under appeal and has not become final.

In all cases the Board has the power to extend these time limits.

Claims and withdrawals of claims must be made by way of entry in a corporation tax return (or amended return) and should be quantified at the time the claim is made. Claims may only be expressed as conditional where the assessment has not been agreed after six years and in circumstances where the conditions are relevant to the determination of the corporation tax assessment and are specified in the claim.

The new rules will require companies to claim capital allowances in the same way as individuals rather than to receive them automatically. Consequently, legislation permitting a company to disclaim capital allowances will be made redundant from the day appointed for the introduction of pay and file.

39

ADMINISTRATION AND COLLECTION

Inspector and collector S.104

This section amends the TMA to make it clear that the Board may allocate duties under the Taxes Acts to any officers as the Board sees fit.

Recovery of excessive tax repayments S.105

From 26 July 1990 assessments to recover excessive repayments of tax will be made under the general assessing machinery rather than the special provisions for recovery. This is necessary because of differences in the interest rules for the two provisions under pay and file.

Corporation tax collection S.106

Corporation tax due under pay and file is to be treated for the purposes of recovery and collection as if it were due and payable by assessment on the company.

40

SPECIAL BUSINESSES
BANKS AND BUILDING SOCIETIES

Debts of overseas governments, etc S. 74

Special provisions are introduced to modify the normal rules for allowance of relief for bad and doubtful foreign debts by spreading the relief and thus smoothing the impact on the Exchequer. They apply to periods of account ending on or after 20 March 1990 and have their main impact on banks.

The debts affected by the new provisions are debts owed or guaranteed by an overseas state authority, the definition of which is extended to include central banks, public or local authorities and similar bodies. In Committee the scope of the legislation was expanded to include private sector debts rendered doubtful through restrictions imposed by overseas laws or government action. Interest on a debt is not within the scope of the Section, nor are debts representing consideration for the provision of goods or services.

Regulations are to be made by the Treasury whereby a maximum percentage of allowable debt will be calculated for any period of account. The Financial Secretary confirmed that these will broadly follow the Bank of England matrix, though producing a point for each country rather than a range. Objective criteria will be established for indicating the likelihood of repayment, apparently by reference to the borrower's inability or unwillingness to meet obligations, with evidence of current difficulties in meeting these and evidence regarding likely future trends also taken into account.

In face of objections to the concept of the Treasury in effect deciding the format of the legislation the Financial Secretary revealed that a draft will be published for consultation and that the regulations will be brought before the House and subject to the affirmative procedure. In relation to the private sector element of the debt the Revenue will apparently publish guidelines on maximum allowances but matrix level relief is not guaranteed.

The regulations will be applied firstly to the last period of account ending before 20 March 1990 (the base period) to give a base percentage. If for a period of account ending less than two years after the base period the percentage is greater than the base percentage, the lower base percentage will be used to give a limit of relief.

If for any subsequent period of account the percentage is greater than the base percentage increased by 5 % for each complete year other than the first since the end of the base period, the limit of relief is the base percentage. In other words, even relief for the modified matrix figure will be restricted if overall deterioration in value of the sovereign debt since the end of the base period is greater than 5 % per annum. Moreover, although this is not explicitly stated, relief will be restricted to the amount provided in the accounts, if this is less than the formula figure. Where the Treasury regulations yield a smaller percentage than was allowed for an earlier period in respect of debts estimated to be bad, it seems that the difference could be added back in the computation of profits.

Where a company had no periods of account ending before 20 March 1990 a notional accounting period will be assumed in calculating the base percentage limits of relief.

There are further provisions restricting relief for realised losses where a deduction has been claimed in an earlier accounting period in respect of debts considered to be bad or doubtful. Unless the disposal of the debt is to the overseas State authority which made the borrowing, there is a limit to the amount of relief which may be claimed in respect of the loss, being 5 % of the debt for the period of account in which the loss is incurred. The balance unallowed may be allowed for subsequent periods of account to a maximum of 5 % of the debt for each complete year since the period of disposal. It is not always clear how this restriction will work in conjunction with the rules relating to provisions.

In Committee the limitation on relief for realised losses was extended as an anti-avoidance measure to debts acquired on or after 20 March 1990 at more than market value.

Though rejecting Opposition proposals for relief in respect of gifts of debts to approved charities for development purposes in Third World countries and pointing out that gifts in kind would not represent allowable expenses of the donor's trade, the Financial Secretary indicated that the relinquishing of debt could be structured to represent charitable donations. These might then be tax-deductible within the 3 % of dividends limit under Section 339 TA.

Abolition of composite rate tax S.30 & Sch.5

As explained in *11: Composite rate tax*, the existing provisions relating to the payment of interest by building societies, banks and other deposit takers are repealed from April 6, 1991. They are replaced from that date by a system of deduction of tax at source under which the tax deducted can be repaid. There will also be special provisions to enable certain investors to self-certify to the deposit taker that they are unlikely to be liable to their tax and are accordingly entitled to be paid interest without deduction of tax.

The provisions for building societies are drafted separately from those for banks and other deposit takers (which will now include local authorities). There are transitional provisions for building societies which pay or credit interest after 28 February 1991 and before 6 April 1991.

Building societies   The new provisions for building societies enable the Inland Revenue to make regulations for the deduction of income tax from dividends and interest paid or credited by building societies. The regulations have not yet been published, but the Inland Revenue are committed to ensuring, after consultation with the building societies, that there is a fully operational system in place well before 6 April 1991. The regulations will include arrangements for the payment of tax deducted, information powers and (a point of major importance to small investors) the means by which certain investors will be able to declare that they are unlikely to be liable to tax and may accordingly be paid interest gross.

Banks and other   The new provisions for banks and other deposit takers seek to achieve the same
deposit takers   effect as described above for building societies, but more detail is contained in the Act, and less is left to regulations. The income tax deducted from interest paid or credited on relevant deposits is to be paid to the Inland Revenue under the existing CT61 procedures that will be familiar to most companies. The Inland Revenue may by regulation exempt interest from deduction of tax, and in particular may provide for the supply of a certificate by the person beneficially entitled to a payment of interest certifying that he is unlikely to be liable to pay any income tax for the year of assessment in which the payment is made.

The definition of 'relevant deposit' (those within the new arrangements) for banks and other deposit takers generally follows the existing definition for composite rate tax (S.481 ICTA). However, whereas certificates of deposit and time deposits of £50,000 or more were only excluded from composite rate tax if they were for a fixed period of at least 7 days, such deposits will now be excluded from income tax deduction if they are for a fixed term of no more than 5 years. This brings the entitlement for banks and other deposit takers to make gross payments into line with the existing position for building societies.

Implementation   The new provisions apply to interest paid or credited on or after April 6, 1991 and include a number of technical adjustments to existing statutory provisions relating to interest paid under deduction of tax, including an obligation on deposit takers to provide investors with certificates of tax deducted.

S.92   The existing powers which the Inland Revenue has to seek information from deposit takers on interest paid are extended to enable the Revenue to prescribe by regulation further information which may be required, and to request books, documents and other records. This has proved controversial, and the Economic Secretary has given an assurance that these powers would not be used to conduct 'fishing operations' amongst customers' accounts.

41
SPECIAL BUSINESSES
OIL INDUSTRY

Allowance for
abandonment
expenditure
S.60

A 100% corporation tax allowance is available to persons carrying on a ring fence trade for expenditure incurred to comply wholly or substantially with an abandonment programme for the closing down of an oil field, and on the demolition of offshore installations or submarine pipelines.

The allowance is available for expenditure, net of any scrap receipts, incurred in a chargeable period ending after 30 June 1991 and must be claimed by irrevocable election within two years of the end of the chargeable period. The election can be made in respect of part or all of the qualifying expenditure and, to the extent the election is not made, allowances under the normal 25% pa reducing balance basis for plant and machinery are available.

It is not clear precisely what 'wholly and substantially in connection with an abandonment programme' means and whether for instance the relief will be available if the Secretary of State requires toppling to a certain depth but the participators want to remove a platform completely. As the relief is linked to demolition costs it is likely that some closing down costs will not qualify and all onshore costs are definitely excluded.

Post-cessation
abandonment
expenditure
S.60

Where a person ceases to carry on a ring fence trade, expenditure incurred after 30 June 1991, provided it is incurred within three years of ceasing that trade, which would have qualified for the 100% allowance referred to above had the trade not ceased, will be included in the pool of plant and machinery allowances under Sections 24 and 25 CAA 1990 (formerly S.44 FA 1971). Qualifying expenditure for these purposes is net of any scrap receipts, and it is not clear whether the full three years must elapse before relief for such costs is available. As the relief is linked to the new 100% abandonment allowance the same restrictions, e.g. exclusion of onshore costs, apply.

Extended carry
back of losses
S.61

To the extent a trading loss is created or enhanced by abandonment expenditure for which a 100% allowance as referred to above is claimed, that loss can be carried back against any income in the preceding three years. This carry back is therefore available against both ring and non-ring fence income and capital gains, and is made automatically as part of a Section 393 (2) TA 1988 carry back election. Thus, relief will firstly be available against total profits of the preceding period of similar length and then against any profits in earlier periods.

Corporation tax	Petroleum Revenue Tax (PRT) is an allowable expense for corporation tax
treatment of	purposes. There is also an unlimited period of carry back of PRT losses which
PRT repayment	would have led to corporation tax computations having to be reopened many
S.62	years after they were 'agreed'. For PRT losses accruing in chargeable periods

Corporation tax treatment of PRT repayment S.62

Petroleum Revenue Tax (PRT) is an allowable expense for corporation tax purposes. There is also an unlimited period of carry back of PRT losses which would have led to corporation tax computations having to be reopened many years after they were 'agreed'. For PRT losses accruing in chargeable periods ending after 30 June 1991 any PRT repayment resulting from a loss carry back shall be chargeable to corporation tax in the accounting period in which the chargeable period in which the relevant PRT loss accrued, ended. Where losses are carried back from two or more PRT chargeable periods which end in different corporation tax accounting periods, and give rise to a repayment in respect of the same PRT chargeable period, the repayment is apportioned between the two corporation tax accounting periods in an appropriate manner.

Disposals of shares deriving their value from UK oil assets S.63

For disposals from 22 January 1990 of shares or securities which, on 31 March 1982 were unquoted and derived most of their value from UK or UK Continental Shelf oil rights or assets, it will no longer be possible to include such assets in an election under Section 96(5) FA 88, in order to compute the gain only by reference to the March 1982 market value. A comparison must therefore always be made of the gain or loss by reference to original cost and the gain or loss by reference to the March 1982 market value.

If an election under Section 96(5) FA 1988 has already been made before 22 January 1990, although not normally revocable, it will be possible to revoke such an election before 1 January 1991 if the company or group held shares as described above at the time the election was made.

Limitation of losses on disposal of oil industry assets S.64

For certain oil industry assets it will not be possible to enhance a capital loss with an indexation allowance based on the March 1982 market value if the disposal takes place on or after 22 January 1990. The assets affected are:

- UK oil licences;

- shares and securities which were unquoted and derived most of their value from UK oil rights and assets on 31 March 1982;

- non-mobile assets used in exploration or exploitation of the UK or the UK Continental Shelf; *and*

- mobile assets similarly used and dedicated to a UK oil field.

The new provisions apply where the calculations of the capital gain by reference to cost and March 1982 market value (using indexation on the March 1982 value in both cases) both give rise to a loss. Normally the lower loss would be the available loss but for disposals as described above a third calculation must be done computing the gain or loss using the original cost and indexation on the original cost of the asset. If this third calculation produces a loss that is the allowable loss. If it produces a gain or neither a gain nor a loss, then the asset is deemed to have been acquired for a consideration that gives rise to neither a gain nor a loss on the disposal.

This provision will have no effect if the 'normal' calculations produce a taxable gain or a deemed 'no gain no loss' situation, and there is, therefore, no restriction in using March 1982 values or indexation thereon to reduce a capital gain.

Limit on PRT interest where loss carried back S. 121

If a PRT loss is carried back from a chargeable period ending after 30 June 1991 and gives rise to a repayment of PRT, there is a limit to the amount of interest supplement that can accrue on that repayment. The limit is that the PRT repayment plus any interest thereon cannot exceed 85% of the loss which gives rise to that repayment. The provision is designed to ensure that the combined PRT, corporation tax and royalty repayments plus interest thereon cannot exceed expenditures incurred in generating those repayments.

Variation of expenditure claim decisions resulting from fraud or negligence S. 122

Provisions exist for the Revenue to reopen decisions on expenditure claims within three years of the decision if it appears that the amount determined as allowable or qualifying for supplement was incorrect. These provisions are now extended such that the three-year time limit is excluded if there has been an overstatement of the amount allowable as the result of fraudulent or negligent conduct, either resulting in an error in statements or declarations made in respect of the decision, or in not immediately notifying the Revenue of any innocent error. This extension of the time limit for reopening decisions is to be applied retroactively to all claim decisions whenever made.

Gas levy S. 123

The gas levy was introduced to enhance Government tax take from gas produced which was exempt from PRT by virtue of the grandfathering provisions put in place when PRT was introduced in 1975.

The interaction of the gas levy legislation and the PRT exemption provisions following the introduction of the Gas Act 1986 meant that in certain circumstances gas production could be subject to PRT and the gas levy. Section 123 is designed to ensure that the gas levy will not be applied where the value of the production is subject to PRT and is to be applied retroactively from 24 August 1986, the date British Gas was privatised.

42 SPECIAL BUSINESSES
INSURANCE COMPANIES AND FRIENDLY SOCIETIES

FA 1989 contained wholesale reforms of the way in which the corporation tax liabilities of life assurance companies are computed. Most of the new provisions were to take effect from 1 January 1990. However, following representations from the life industry some of the provisions are substantially amended in, or never have effect as a result of, the Finance Act. In addition completely new provisions are introduced largely to complete the reform process and to tidy up some loose ends.

Apportionment of income, etc S.41 & Sch.6

Under the old régime for taxing life companies investment income, capital gains and business profits attributable to different classes of business were apportioned on the basis of the respective mean of the opening and closing liabilities to pay benefits to policy holders and annuitants, or possibly by reference to respective mean long-term business funds. A new Section 432A introduces with effect from 1 January 1990 a revised and more specific basis for allocating income and capital gains or losses to the following categories of business:

- pension business;

- general annuity business;

- overseas life assurance business (broadly business done with non-resident policy holders and annuitants through an overseas branch of a UK life company); *and*

- basic life assurance business (being life assurance business other than the preceding three categories). For this purpose industrial assurance business is distinguished from ordinary long-term business.

The first step in the allocation process is to attribute income from, and gains arising on the disposal of, assets linked solely to the various categories of business or assets of the overseas life assurance fund.

The second step is to allocate the balance of income and gains between categories of business.

Assets not directly attributed through step one are allocated in the ratio that the average of opening and closing liabilities within the category of business, plus the average of the appropriate part of opening and closing investment reserve, bears to the total of mean opening and closing liabilities and investment reserve, after exclusion in all cases of directly attributed assets. The appropriate part of the investment reserve, excluding the overseas life element, is calculated by comparing the with-profits liabilities of each category of business with total with-profits liabilities. However, where all the liabilities are linked liabilities or all, except perhaps an insignificant proportion, are non-linked without profits liabilities, the allocation of the reserve is by reference to the relative proportion of such linked or non-linked liabilities.

New Sections 432 B-E TA introduce similar rules for allocating between categories of business elements in the revenue account prepared for the purposes of the Insurance Companies Act 1982 which are required by Section 83 FA 1989 to be brought into account where profits of a class of life assurance business are calculated on a Case I of Schedule D basis.

Where separate revenue accounts are prepared for parts of the business these will be used in apportioning for this purpose.

New Section 432C governs apportionment of investment income in the case of funds with no participating policy holders. Income from assets linked solely to particular categories of business and income from assets designated as overseas life business assets is first identified and the balance of income is again attributed on the basis of mean opening and closing liabilities less the value of assets linked to a particular category of business.

New Section 432D applies a similar basis of apportionment to the increase or decrease over the accounting period in the value of assets of funds without participating policy holders.

New Section 432E provides for apportionment of the sum of investment income and movements in the value of assets attributable to funds in which some policy holders are entitled to participate. There are two bases of calculation and the one yielding the greater amount applies. Under the first basis, except in the case of a mutual company where there is no allocation, the unallocated surplus (as per form 58 of the DTI return) disclosed by a particular revenue account is divided between categories of business in the same ratio as actual allocations to give an allocation of the whole of the surplus. This share of unallocated surplus represents in effect the year's profit from the particular category of business, except in the case of a mutual company where no part of the unallocated surplus is attributed to the annuity business computations. The allocation in turn enables the relevant aggregate income and investment appreciation (the aggregate) to be calculated for the purpose of the second test.

This second test ensures a minimum return on investments in the particular category by substituting for the aggregate, where appropriate, a figure of income and appreciation made up by combining:

a) the actual return from assets linked solely to a particular category of business; *and*

b) a notional investment return based on a statutory percentage set by the Treasury and based on the average gross redemption yield on 15-year higher coupon British Government stocks, as published in the Financial Times, applied to mean liabilities, less the linked assets, for each category of business.

Where for any category or categories of business the amount under the second basis is the greater and therefore is substituted, thus increasing the surplus, the amount determined under the first basis is to be reduced pro rata for the rest of the categories of business, so that the total allocations to all categories will not create total profits in excess of the actual surplus. In applying the second test there is a safeguard, which has regard to the overall return on investments for the particular company, to ensure that this reallocation could not create a greater imputed investment return in total than the actual return.

There are additional provisions for attributing income to overseas life business and in particular to take account of the special treatment of UK dividends received.

The rest of Schedule 6 comprises miscellaneous amendments to existing legislation to take account of Finance Act changes and provisions to cover transfers of assets within and out of and into the long-term business fund.

Transfers of assets, etc   The identification rules described above require rules for dealing with transfers of assets between categories of business and Section 440 TA, which allowed such transfers without tax effect, is replaced. From 1 January 1990 transfers into or out of five separate categories of asset involve a notional disposal and reacquisition at market value. The categories are:

a) assets linked solely to basic life assurance business (i.e. excluding *b)* and *c)* below and assets linked to the general annuity business);

b) assets linked solely to pension business;

c) assets of the overseas life fund;

d) other assets of the long-term business fund; *and*

e) other assets (outside of the long-term business fund).

Moreover, the facility to transfer assets for capital gains purposes within a group without immediate gain or loss is removed, effectively ring-fencing the long-term fund. (Special rules apply to the transfer of a life assurance business.)

For CGT purposes there are consequential provisions for treating single holdings of securities of a particular class as separate holdings referable to each of the above five categories and for attributing the securities to each category.

Furthermore, where appropriate, these separate holdings are to be divided as at 1 January 1990 between the 1982 holding and the separate new holding elements, as defined in Schedule 19 FA 1985. The legislation does not in terms deal with the treatment of 1965 holdings.

There are transitional provisions relating to 1982 and new holdings to take into account the fact that the new provisions do not necessarily take effect on 1 January 1990.

Section 88 F(No 2)A 1975, which lays down rules for identification of disposals of shareholdings of 2% or more for CGT purposes, ceases to apply to life companies.

Overseas life assurance business S.42 & Sch.7

The former provisions in Section 441 TA governing the treatment of the 'foreign life fund' element of the business of a UK life insurance company, and providing a measure of exemption from taxation of relevant income and gains, are replaced by new provisions for accounting periods beginning on or after 1 January 1990.

Under these the profits of the overseas life business, computed as if it were a separate trade under the rules of Case I of Schedule D, are taxable under Case VI of Schedule D. The computation is under the extended rules in FA 1989 applicable to pension and annuity business profits. In addition referable interest and annuities are deductible.

However, losses may only be carried forward against similar profits and cannot be set off against other Case VI profits. Relevant management expenses and capital allowances on machinery or plant used for management of the overseas business are deductible in the Case I computation rather than in the I-E computation (a special basis of computation which applies to the income and gains attributable to the basic life assurance business of a company). Because they are a component of the Case VI computation, investment income and capital gains attributable to the overseas business are not chargeable to tax as such and separate exemptions, as were provided in old Section 441, are not necessary.

Franked investment income deriving from assets of an overseas life fund may be included in the computation but there is no tax credit in respect of such a distribution except to the extent that an individual resident in the territory where the relevant branch is situated would be entitled to relief under the terms of a double taxation treaty. There are detailed rules for relating assets to overseas branches for this purpose and restriction of relief in respect of certain reinsurance business elements. Where tax credit is available it is repayable to the company but the relevant gross dividend cannot be used to frank dividends paid.

The rules in Schedule 6 for attributing income and gains to categories of business for the purposes of a Case I computation are amended slightly to take into account the special treatment of distributions.

Credit for overseas tax paid on profits of the overseas life business against corporation tax payable on such profits is restricted to the shareholders' share of the overseas tax. Very broadly, relief is restricted if the Case I profits chargeable under new Section 441 are less than the income less expenses element. Any restriction of credit relief is allowed by deduction in computing profits.

There are detailed rules for determining what are assets of the overseas life assurance fund and how long they remain in that fund.

There is an initial attribution of assets to the overseas life fund and at the end of each subsequent period a comparison will be made between:

A: the value of the assets which have been assets of the fund in the period; *and*

B: the aggregate of the liabilities of the overseas fund at the end of the accounting period and the appropriate part of the investment reserve calculated by reference to mean liabilities using the same basis of allocation as for attribution of income and gains laid down in Section 432A.

Any shortfall of A against B will occasion a deemed acquisition into the overseas fund during or at the end of the accounting period and any excess will occasion a similar disposal.

These deemed transfers will be satisfied out of the following categories of assets in order of precedence as stated:

a) assets linked solely to overseas life business;

b) foreign currency assets matching liabilities to pay benefits in the same currency;

c) assets under the control of a person working out of the overseas branch;

d) UK and local government securities issued on free-of-tax terms to non-residents ('FOTRA' securities);

e)   assets other than UK equities; *and*

f)   UK equities.

Deduction for
policy holders' tax
S. 43

Section 82 FA 1989 is amplified to make it clear that amounts allocated to or expended on behalf of policy holders or annuitants, deductible in computing profits on a Case I basis, include relevant foreign tax and, except in the case of general annuity, pension and overseas life business, the policy holders' share of UK tax on investment income and gains.

Reinsurance
commissions
S. 44

It is made clear that reinsurance commissions received are not to be included in receipts of the basic life assurance business which are treated as separately chargeable under Case VI of Schedule D.

Such commissions earned referable to basic life assurance business are to be deducted from allowable management expenses but they may be used to limit the amount of acquisition expenses which are subject to spreading over seven years.

In all cases the reinsurance commissions in question relate only to amounts received in respect of liabilities assumed in respect of insurances made on or after 14 March 1989 or variations after that date of policies issued before 14 March.

Policy holders'
share of profits, etc
S. 45

The special rate of corporation tax for life assurance companies only applies to the policy holders' share of profits, the shareholders' share being charged at the full corporation tax rate. The rules in FA 1989 for allocating investment income, gains and profits for this purpose did not work and are replaced from the outset (ie from 1 January 1990) by new rules.

Section 88 FA 1989, as amended, makes it clear that in the case of a mutual company the whole of the profits will be treated as belonging to policy holders.

The new Section 89 FA 1989 defines the policy holders' share of the life business taxable profits as the balance, if any, after the shareholders' share has been calculated in the following way.

The shareholders' share begins with the Case I profit of the company i.e. the profit which would emerge if its total operation were taxed on the basis of the Case I of Schedule D rules (including the special rules for life companies in Sections 82 and 83 FA 1989). From this figure is first deducted the unrelieved amount of any franked investment income (FII) in respect of which an election has been made under Section 438(6) TA (to exclude certain FII from the computation of pension business profits).

Finally the shareholders' share of non-pension business FII is deducted to yield the net shareholders' share of total profits. This share of FII is calculated using a fraction of A over B where A is the company's Case I profits and B the amount by which the sum of investment income and increase (or decrease) in value of investments exceeds expenses, the figures being taken from form 40 of the DTI return. Where expenses in B exceed income or where A exceeds B, the whole of the FII is treated as shareholders' share. Where A is nil, none of the FII is shareholders' unless expenses in B exceed income.

This same allocation of FII between shareholders and policy holders is used in the restriction in franking distributions to the shareholders' share of FII.

The new definition of policy holders' share of total profits is used in the restriction of the set-off of ACT against corporation tax profits and in the similar restriction of set-off of group relief and losses.

The facility to exclude FII from the pension business Case VI computation by election up to the amount of the profit is now restricted to the shareholders' share of the FII.

Annual deemed disposal of holdings of unit trusts, etc S. 46 & Sch. 8

For capital gains tax purposes there will be a deemed disposal and reacquisition at market value at the end of the accounting period of rights under an authorised unit trust and of certain interests in offshore funds held as part of the assets of the long-term business fund. Originally these provisions were to apply to accounting periods commencing on or after 1 January 1991. Following representations, provision is made for the Treasury by order to put back the operative date until after the abolition of stamp duty on securities (possibly close to 31 December 1991), this with the intention of permitting companies to avoid the duty when they replace assets within the charge.

These provisions do not apply to assets linked only to pension business or forming part of the overseas life fund and there are rules for identifying assets which are not linked solely to particular classes of business. These rules again use relevant mean liabilities to first identify those parts of unit trust holdings, etc which are linked or specifically identified assets and which are not chargeable on a Case I or Case VI basis and then make a similar identification in relation to non-linked assets.

Schedule 8 provides for transitional relief from the effects of Section 46 on a claim made within two years of the end of an accounting period.

The operation of the charge may be deferred to the extent that it would relate to assets held in connection with investment-linked policies made before 1 April 1990 and not subsequently varied. Relevant liabilities are to be monitored at the end of each accounting period and the election will not apply to the extent that there are reductions in corresponding liabilities, although a margin in favour of the company is built into the formula.

The effect of the part disposal rules is to erode the value of this relief more quickly than the run-off of liabilities would warrant. The Government has promised to consider detailed amending legislation next year.

The Section 46 charge may also be deferred where new assets are acquired to replace Section 46 assets if these new assets would give rise to chargeable gains on disposal. Reinvestment has to be made within six months of disposal and a claim has to be made within two years of the end of the accounting period in which the exchange occurs. Again there are matching provisions to ensure that replacement assets are truly attributable to Section 46 assets.

The provisions apply with appropriate amendments to transfer of long-term business under a scheme sanctioned by a court under Section 49 Insurance Companies Act 1982.

Spreading of gains and losses under Section 46 S.47

Chargeable gains and allowable losses arising on deemed disposals under the provisions of Section 46 as at the end of an accounting period are to be aggregated. Only one-seventh of any aggregate gain or loss will be charged or allowed immediately, the balance being spread over subsequent accounting periods until the whole amount has been accounted for.

If a net loss arises on the deemed disposals at the end of an accounting period a claim may be made within two years of the end of this accounting period to carry back all or part of the loss against net gains of the preceding six accounting periods, the set-off being against the gains of the latest accounting period first.

Transfers of long-term business S.48 & Sch.9

Where there is a scheme for transfer of all or part of the life assurance or other long-term business of a company approved by a court under Section 49 Insurance Companies Act 1982 (a transfer) these new provisions provide for transfers of reliefs and deferral of charges which would otherwise not be available under the provisions of the Taxes Acts. A transfer causes the accounting period of the transferring company to end with the day of the transfer.

The new provisions, as set out below, confirm and extend the concessional treatment announced in a Revenue Press Release in October 1988 and apply to transfers on or after 1 January 1990.

1. The relief from CGT charge afforded by Section 267 TA 1970 in relation to company reconstructions and amalgamations is not prevented from applying to a transfer merely because it is not a reconstruction, etc as defined, or because the transfer is not between two UK resident companies, and it applies to assets which are technically stock in trade. The relief only extends to assets which would be chargeable assets on a disposal at the time of the transfer. The relief does not permit the transferor to pass unused CGT losses to the transferee.

2. Similar exemption from immediate charge is extended to the CGT charge which would otherwise arise on the cessation of a trade carried on in the UK through a branch or agency.

3. Management expenses which would have been allowed to the transferor in subsequent accounting periods are treated as management expenses of the transferee, with appropriate application of the spreading and other provisions relating to such expenses in FA 1989. This major relief did not figure in the published concessions referred to above.

4. Similarly losses which would have been allowed to the transferor, if the relevant business had continued, go to the transferee where the losses arise from the computation of profit of general annuity or pension business or under the new rules of computation relating to overseas life business.

5. Balancing allowances or charges under CAA 1990 are not brought about by the transfer and the transferee is entitled to allowances and liable to charges which would have fallen to be made to or on the transferor.

The provisions do not apply if the transfer is not made for bona fide commercial reasons and has avoidance of corporation tax as a purpose.

A transfer to a friendly society from an insurance company does not carry with it the normal title to tax exemption held by the friendly society.

Friendly societies: increased tax exemption S.49

The maximum size of contracts issued by a friendly society without it losing tax exemption on the profits from the relevant business is increased from £100 per person to £150. Opposition attempts to increase the limit still further to £900 were unsuccessful.

S.50

The Treasury is given power to make regulations to apply the provisions of the Taxes Acts relating to transfers of long-term business, with necessary adaptations, to transfers between friendly societies or from a friendly society to a company which is not a friendly society.

43
SPECIAL BUSINESSES
UNIT AND INVESTMENT TRUSTS AND PENSIONS SCHEMES

Authorised unit
trusts
S.51

With effect from 1 January 1990 income of an authorised unit trust which is freely marketable within the EC has been assessable to corporation tax at a lower rate equal to the basic rate of income tax. From 1 January 1991 *all* authorised unit trusts will enjoy the advantage of a corporation tax rate for the financial year equal to income tax at the basic rate for the year beginning 6 April in the financial year concerned.

The reduction will apply to income of accounting periods ending after 31 December 1990 e.g. from 1 January 1991 where an accounting period of the trustees of an authorised trust which is not freely marketable in the EC starts on that date. Where an accounting period straddles 31 December 1990 the new reduced rate rule will apply to so much of the period as falls in the 1991 financial year. Furthermore, so much of the period as falls between 1 January 1991 and 31 March 1991 will be charged at 25%.

A few unit trusts investing in gilts or sterling deposits pay income tax at the basic rate but get no relief for their management expenses or interest paid. With effect from the first distribution period of such a trust starting after 31 December 1990, relief will be given for interest on borrowings permitted under DTI regulations and for management expenses.

Changes are also made to the treatment of income from authorised unit trusts received by corporate investors. In relation to dividends of a distribution period ending after 31 December 1990, a recipient within the charge to corporation tax, not being a dual resident, will be treated as receiving an annual payment under deduction of basic rate income tax in respect of so much of the dividend as relates to the period from 1 January 1991. Excluded from this treatment are unit trust managers holding units in the ordinary course of their business and authorised trusts investing in other trusts. The position of a small number of investment trusts at least 90% of whose investments were, on Budget day, in authorised unit trusts is also protected, and if the conditions of the newly inserted Section 468G TA are satisfied, distributions received by such an investment trust will continue to be treated as franked investment income.

Life assurance companies are the main corporate investors in authorised unit trusts. Their rate of corporation tax on income and capital gains attributable to policy holders is the basic rate of income tax. The new regime for taxing the distributions of authorised unit trusts will mean that corporation tax on such income attributable to policy holders will be covered by tax credited.

S.52   Certain existing provisions are repealed as a consequence of the Section 51 provisions.

Exemption from bond-washing provisions S.53   Unit trust managers are exempted from the rules against bond-washing (i.e. the conversion of income into capital gains by selling units prior to an ex-dividend date) in respect of transactions in the units in the trusts they manage which are in the ordinary course of their business. This gives unit trust managers the same exemption as stock exchange market makers enjoy for other types of security. The exemption applies for the past as well as the future.

Indexation: collective investment schemes S.54   The CGT indexation allowance has been due on units in unit trusts and offshore funds that are invested mainly in assets (for example gilts or building society shares) which would not themselves qualify for the allowance.

In relation to disposals on or after 20 March 1990 of rights in property to which collective investment arrangements relate (i.e. arrangements which constitute a collective investment scheme as defined in Section 75(1) FSA), indexation relief will not be granted if, at some time in the relevant period of ownership (i.e. the period beginning with the later of 1 April 1982 and the earliest date on which consideration was given for the rights and ending with the date of disposal), not less than 90% of the market value at any time of investment property (i.e. all property except cash awaiting investment) then falling within the arrangements was represented by:

- assets which if they were disposed of at the same time as the rights would not be liable to capital gains tax; *or*

- shares in a building society.

Investment trusts S.55   One of the conditions of the Board approving a company as an investment trust is that not more than 15% of the income of an accounting period derived from shares and securities is retained. This rule is to be relaxed in relation to accounting periods ending on or after 26 July 1990 where:

a)   the company is required by law to retain an amount greater than 15% of its income from shares and securities; *or*

b)   the amount which the company would be required to distribute in order to comply with the 15% test would be less than £10,000 for a 12-month accounting period.

Pension schemes and authorised unit trusts are exempt from tax on capital gains but not on trading income. In some circumstances futures and options transactions might be deemed to constitute trading. Section 81 provides that all income from futures and options (irrespective of whether they are traded on an exchange or settled in cash or otherwise) will be exempt from tax in the hands of pension schemes and unit trusts.

So far as authorised unit trusts are concerned, trustees of such a trust are exempted from tax under Case I of Schedule D on income from futures contracts and options contracts.

As to pension schemes, the meaning of 'investments' (income from which is tax exempt) is widened to include futures contracts and options contracts.

The intention of the legislation is not only to remove uncertainty about the eligibility of income from futures and options for tax exemption but also to assist futures and options funds (a new type of authorised unit trust) to get off the ground when the necessary DTI and SIB regulations are made.

44

SPECIAL BUSINESSES
WASTE DISPOSAL

Two new sections are added to the Taxes Act in order to provide relief for expenditure incurred in preparing and making good waste disposal sites. On 6 April 1989 the Court of Appeal held in the case of Rolfe v Wimpey Waste Management Limited that in acquiring landfill sites and incurring expenditure upon their preparation and subsequent restoration, what the taxpayer company had acquired was a capital asset and accordingly such expenditure was not deductible in computing taxable profits. Prior to that decision the Revenue had, in practice, usually allowed the costs of site preparation and restoration to be deducted in computing profits for tax purposes but, unfortunately, it had been conceded in the Wimpey case that the question of the allowability of such expenditure stood or fell by reference to the decision on the central question of whether landfill sites were fixed or current assets.

Consequent upon that decision the waste management industry (advised by Ernst & Young) made representations to the Government and to the Inland Revenue with a view to obtaining a change in the law. Whilst the Treasury strongly resisted proposals for a form of relief in respect of the cost of acquiring airspace (i.e. for the 'premium' paid over and above the existing use value of land for the right to tip on that land), it was conceded that the decision in the Wimpey case went further than was intended and so provisions have been introduced with a view to restoring the status quo post Wimpey.

S. 78   New Section 91A provides that a site restoration payment made on or after 6 April 1989 will be deductible for tax purposes for the period of account in which the payment is made. A site restoration payment is a payment made in connection with the restoration of a site or part of a site and in order to comply with any condition of a relevant licence or any condition imposed on the grant of planning permission to use the site for waste disposal activities, or under a relevant agreement made under section 52 Town and Country Planning Act 1971 (or the comparable provisions in Scotland and Northern Ireland).

A relevant licence is either a disposal licence under the Control of Pollution Act 1974 or a waste management licence under the new Environmental Protection Act 1990 (or the corresponding provisions in Northern Ireland). Waste disposal activities include the collection, treatment, conversion and final depositing of waste materials.

No relief will be given in respect of expenditure which has previously been allowed as a deduction or in respect of which capital allowances have or may be made. It should also be noted that relief is to be given on a payments, rather than an accruals, basis.

New section 91B provides that in computing the profits of a trade for a period of account ending after 5 April 1989, the 'allowable amount' of any site preparation expenditure will be deductible for tax purposes provided:

a) it is incurred by a person in the course of carrying on a trade in relation to a waste disposal site (the site in question);

b) a relevant licence is held by that person at the time when waste materials are first deposited on the site in question; *and*

c) a claim is made for relief supported by such plans and documents as the Board may require.

It is immaterial whether expenditure is incurred before or after the coming into force of this section.

A period of account is a period for which an account is made up. Site preparation expenditure is defined as expenditure on preparing the site for deposit of waste materials and may include expenditure on earthworks, and relevant licence has the same meaning as for section 91A. The Revenue have indicated that a site will be regarded as the land comprised in a relevant licence.

The 'allowable amount' in relation to a period of account will be determined in accordance with the formula:

$$A - B \times \frac{C}{C + D}$$

where:

A = site preparation expenditure incurred by the person at any time prior to or during the period in question in relation to the site in question and in the course of carrying on the trade, but excluding any expenditure:

a) previously allowed (otherwise than under these provisions) as a deduction in computing profits for any preceding period; *or*
b) which constitutes capital expenditure in respect of which capital allowances have or may be made.

B = the aggregate amount allowed as a deduction under these provisions in computing the profits of the trade for any preceding periods of account in relation to the site in question;

C = the volume of waste materials deposited on the site in question during the period in question, except that in the case of a period beginning before 6 April 1989, C will exclude the volume of waste materials deposited during the period prior to that date; *and*

D = the unused capacity of the site in question (in terms of volume) at the end of the period in question.

However, where any expenditure which would fall to be included in A (because it has not previously been allowed for tax purposes) was incurred before 6 April 1989, A will be reduced by an amount determined by the formula:

$$E \times \frac{F}{F+G}$$

where:

E = so much of the expenditure at A as was incurred before 6 April 1989;

F = the volume of waste materials deposited on the site in question before 6 April 1989; *and*

G = the unused capacity of the site in question (in terms of volume) immediately before 6 April 1989.

This is best explained by an example:

	Periods to 31.12.88	Period to 5.4.89	Period to 31.12.89	Year to 31.12.90
Site preparation costs (all revenue) £000s	300*	30	70	100
Waste deposited 000s cubic metres	450	50	200	400
Unused capacity at end of period, 000s cubic metres	1,050	1,000	800	400

(*assumed all allowed for tax purposes otherwise than under these provisions)

90

Allowable amount for year to 31.12.89

$$A - B \times \frac{C}{C+D}$$

but A will be reduced for this period by an amount equal to

$$E \times \frac{F}{F+G}$$

namely:

$$£30,000 \times \frac{500}{500+1,000} = £10,000$$

A is therefore:

$$£100,000 - £10,000 = £90,000$$

The allowable amount is therefore:

$$(£90,000-0) \times \frac{200}{200+800} = £18,000$$

Allowable amount for the year to 31.12.90

A will again be reduced by the figure of £10,000 as computed above so the calculation will be:

$$(£190,000-£18,000) \times \frac{400}{400+400} = £86,000$$

It will be observed that although the provisions are meant to restore the status quo following the decision in the Wimpey case, there will undoubtedly be expenditure in periods prior to 6 April 1989 which, because assessments were still open at that date, will now be disallowed. The Treasury declined to take on board suggestions that relief be given for such expenditure either by way of statute or concession.

45

SPECIAL BUSINESSES
FOOTBALL SAFETY

S. 4   The rate of pool betting duty is reduced by Section 4 from 42½% to 40%. The new rate applies to bets made at any time in relation to events taking place on or after 6 April 1990.

The reduction in the rate of pool betting duty was announced in the Budget. The Chancellor made it clear that the rate of duty would be reduced only on the condition that the duty lost to the government was given to the Football Trust and was applied in carrying out the safety recommendations made by Lord Justice Taylor in his report on the Hillsborough disaster. Agreement that the tax saved would be so applied was reached on 23 May 1990 by the Football League, the Football Trust and the pools companies.

S. 126   Section 126 ensures that the full effect of the duty reduction benefits football and is not clawed back through other taxes. Consequently Section 126 removes certain income tax, corporation tax and inheritance tax liabilities which might otherwise arise.

Section 126 applies to any payment made in consequence of the reduction in pool betting duty by a person liable to pay that duty in order to meet capital expenditure incurred in improving the safety or comfort of spectators at Football Association grounds and has the following effects:

1.   Any such payments made by a person carrying on a trade may be deducted in computing for tax purposes the profits or gains of that trade.

2.   Such payments do not constitute annual payments.

3.   Such payments are not caught by Section 153 CAA 90 which generally denies capital allowances in respect of otherwise qualifying capital expenditure to the extent that the expenditure incurred by a person is funded by a contribution from any other person.

4.   Where a payment is made to trustees, the sum received by the trustees and any assets representing that sum are not subject to the inheritance tax charge imposed on settlements without an interest in possession.

46

BROADCASTING

S. 80 & Sch. 12 Schedule 12 incorporates measures to facilitate the changes to be introduced by the Broadcasting Act 1990. Under this, the Independent Broadcasting Authority ('IBA') and the Cable Authority will give way to new bodies, namely the Radio Authority, the Independent Television Commission ('ITC') and the new transmission company.

Schedule 12 provides the following:-

a) the new transmission company will be treated as if it had always carried on IBA transmission activities and a proportion of IBA's unallowed tax losses and capital expenditure eligible for capital allowances will be apportioned to it;

b) the transfer of IBA's assets to the ITC and the Radio Authority will, for capital gains tax purposes, be deemed to be for a consideration such that no gain or loss accrues to the IBA. The new company will take over IBA's rights as regards determination of the base cost of the assets (ie. original cost or 31 March 1982 value);

c) the transfer of direct broadcasting by satellite ('DBS') assets by the IBA to a DBS contractor, the transfer of Cable Authority assets to the ITC and the transfer of the shares in the Channel 4 Company from the ITC to the Channel Four Television Corporation will be deemed to be for a consideration such that no gain or loss accrues to the disposing company. The acquiring companies will take over base cost of the asset to the IBA;

d) the unallowed capital losses of the IBA will be apportioned between the new companies; *and*

e) for purposes of the roll-over relief rules which allow deferral of capital gains, the new companies will be treated as if they had owned the assets and used them in the same manner as the IBA.

47

PORTS PRIVATISATION LEVY

Ss.115-120 This is a completely new levy aimed specifically at the privatisation of trust ports. Encouraged by government, two trust port authorities are currently promoting private Bills through Parliament to give them increased powers. The ownership of these trust ports is uncertain, but the government has deemed it appropriate to take a portion of the proceeds when the securities are disposed of. This applies to disposals:

- *by* the port authority, a company under its control or a person constituted under a private Act

- *of* securities in a company which is (or has control of) a company to which all or part of the port authority's undertaking has been transferred under a private Act.

The legislation has been passed with the two private Bills in mind but is intended to be wide enough to catch any reconstruction which achieves the same result i.e. private ownership of a trust port.

This is a levy, not a tax, and is to be administered by the Department of Transport, not by the Inland Revenue. The administration is not governed by the Taxes Management Act and there is no specific appeals procedure. It is understood that the only remedy in the event of dispute with the Secretary of State for Transport regarding the amount of levy due would be a civil action through the courts.

It should be noted that the 50% levy is charged on the value of the company at the time of the disposal which will reflect the value of any right to receive its share of the proceeds. It is accordingly potentially much higher than 50% of the value of the existing undertaking.

S.116 The levy will be charged at the rate of 50% of the consideration or the market value at the time of the disposal if higher. A deduction is allowed for expenses such as professional and valuation fees, advertising, and transfer costs, wholly and exclusively incurred on the disposal. There are anti-avoidance provisions attacking arrangements under which the value of the securities has been materially reduced.

Market value is determined in accordance with the capital gains tax provisions but there is no 'arms length' test necessary. It remains to be seen how this will be applied in practice and whether in fact the market value issue will follow established capital gains tax principles.

The Treasury has power to vary the rate of the levy by statutory instrument approved by the House of Commons.

S.117   To encourage employee participation, up to 3% of the amount on which levy would otherwise be chargeable will be exempt where the securities are transferred for less than market value to employees, directors, share option or share incentive schemes. The allowance is calculated on each disposal and limited to 3% of amounts chargeable up to that time so that it may be important to plan the timing of disposals and defer employee participation.

S.119   Written notification of a disposal to which levy applies must be given to the Secretary of State within 30 days of the disposal. The Secretary of State has powers to call for information and documents from the parties to the transaction, including the company whose securities have been disposed of.

There are penalties for failure to notify or to comply, and for making fraudulent or negligent returns.

S.118   Levy will be assessed by, and is payable to the Secretary of State (for Transport) within 3 months of the disposal or, if later, within 30 days of the date of issue of the assessment notice. Interest on unpaid levy will be charged from the due date. If the levy is not paid within 6 months of the due date it may be recovered from the company whose securities were disposed of.

S.120   The levy is in addition to capital gains tax and is an allowable deduction from the consideration in the computation of any chargeable gain on the disposal of the securities.

Ss. 107-114   Stamp duty and stamp duty reserve tax are to be abolished on transactions in securities with effect from a date to be appointed ('abolition day'). This is likely to be late 1991/92 to coincide with the introduction on The Stock Exchange of paperless dealings. These provisions put into effect the Chancellor's desire expressed in the Budget to encourage wider share ownership and to consolidate London's position as a leading equities market. In the meantime, minor changes have been introduced regarding paired shares and international organisations.

S. 107   Bearer instruments, issued on or after abolition day in the case of UK instruments, or transferred in the UK on or after abolition day in the case of non-UK instruments, are removed from charge.

S. 108   No stamp duty will be chargeable where any of the following securities are transferred to or vested in any person by instrument on or after abolition day:

a)   stocks, shares or loan capital;

b)   interests in, or rights arising out of, stocks, shares or loan capital;

c)   rights or options in respect of, stocks, shares or loan capital; *and*

d)   units under a unit trust scheme.

S. 109   This Section repeals legislation of an administrative nature relating to the stamp duty charge on transactions in securities. These provisions will generally cease to have effect from abolition day but in some cases as provided by Treasury order.

S. 110   Stamp duty reserve tax is also to be abolished in respect of unconditional agreements to transfer securities made on or after abolition day and in respect of conditional agreements made before abolition day whose conditions are satisfied on or after that day.

In regard to the provisions relating to depositary receipts and clearance systems, stamp duty reserve tax is to be abolished in respect of securities issued or transferred on or after abolition day whenever the arrangement was made. Where securities have been issued or transferred prior to abolition day under instalment arrangements stamp duty reserve tax will continue to be chargeable on instalments becoming payable.

S. 111   The abolition day is to be appointed by the Treasury by Statutory Instrument.

Ss. 112 & 113	Where a British company and a foreign company pair their shares in such a way that they can only be transferred as units of one share in each company and such units are offered for public sale in the UK and the foreign country, the units had to be so offered in equal numbers in order to obtain exemption from bearer instrument duty. As this condition cannot very well be satisfied in the case of rights issues because of movements of holdings between the countries concerned, the equal numbers test is now abolished in this regard. At the same time, bonus issues of registered units are brought within the charge to stamp duty reserve tax.
S. 114	This section grants relief from stamp duty reserve tax at 1.5% on the issue of depositary receipts for chargeable securities of designated international organisations and on the provision of clearance services for such chargeable securities.

49 | MISCELLANEOUS
INHERITANCE TAX

Rates 1990-91
SI 1990/680

The threshold for inheritance tax is raised from £118,000 to £128,000 in relation to transfers made on or after 6 April 1990. The rates of tax remain at 40% on cumulative transfers on or within seven years of death (subject to a taper relief) and at 20% for chargeable lifetime dispositions.

Revenue
information
powers
Ss. 124 & 125

The existing wide power (under S.219 IHTA) for the Board to require any person to furnish them with information which they may require for the purposes of the IHTA has been made subject to an application by the Revenue to the Special Commissioners. This provision takes effect with respect to notices given on or after 26 July 1990. This is a limited but welcome restriction although Section 125 extends the scope of such notices to cover taxes of a similar character to inheritance tax imposed under the law of other EC member states (see *36: Information and returns*).

The objective of the latter section is primarily to comply fully with the Directive of the Council of European Communities No 77/799/EEC in respect of other taxes. However, proposed amendments to the Directive in anticipation of the freedom of movement of capital would facilitate the exchange of information on inheritance tax and similar capital taxes, and this enabling provision ensures that immediate compliance is possible on issue by the Treasury of a Statutory Instrument so directing.

50

CUSTOMS AND EXCISE

Alcohol
S. 1

The duty on most alcohol products is increased broadly in line with inflation on goods cleared from 6.00 pm on the day of the Budget, except for the increased excise duty on spirits which represented the first real increase since 1985.

Tobacco
S. 2

With the exception of pipe and chewing tobacco, duties on tobacco products are increased on goods cleared from midnight on 22/23 March. The new rate of excise duty on cigarettes is £34.91 per thousand cigarettes plus 21% of retail price.

Hydrocarbon oil
S. 3

The rates of duty on most hydrocarbon oils are raised and the differential between the taxation of leaded and unleaded petrol increased. The increases are applied to fuel delivered from refineries and bonded warehouses from 6.00 pm on the day of the Budget.

Betting
S. 4

The rate of pool betting duty is reduced to 40% on bets placed on events taking place on or after 28 May (see *45: Football safety*).

Vehicles
Ss. 5-6 &
Sch. 2

The rates of vehicle excise duty and rate bands for certain types of commercial vehicle are adjusted. Section 6 exempts from duty vehicles belonging to voluntary organisations which provide for the needs of disabled people. It also defines the vehicles already exempt as ambulances and exempts pedestrian-controlled vehicles from licensing.

Period entry
S. 7 & Sch. 3

The Customs and Excise Management Act 1979 is amended to enable agents to complete import entries under the simplified period entry scheme. The scheme allows importers of EC goods to submit monthly computerised summaries of goods imported.

Other
Ss. 8 & 9

Section 8 amends the definition of methylated spirits and Section 9 abolishes the requirement that licensed distillers should provide living accommodation for officers in charge of a distillery.

51 | MISCELLANEOUS
SOCIAL SECURITY

The Community Charge Benefits (General) Amendment No. 2 Regulations 1990. SI 1990/835

It was announced in the Budget that the capital limits over which individuals would not be entitled to Community Charge Benefit were to be increased.

The Department of Social Security has made Regulations effective from 1 April 1990 which increase the capital limit from £8,000 to £16,000 and also allow any claims made before 28 May 1990 to be backdated to 1 April 1990 or some later date on which the individual satisfied the relevant benefit entitlement conditions.

The effect of the Regulations means that individuals with capital of more than £16,000 will not be entitled to the benefit but where the capital is less than the upper limit a notional income of £1 a week will be assumed for each £250, or part of £250, between £3,000 and £16,000.

52 | MISCELLANEOUS
MISCELLANEOUS AMENDMENTS

Capital allowances
S.88 & Sch.13

Miscellaneous amendments are introduced generally with effect from 6 April 1990 to correct minor defects of a technical nature which emerged from the CAA consolidation process.

Errors in TA
Sch.14

Miscellaneous amendments are introduced to correct minor errors in TA, TMA, Oil Taxation Act 1975, CGTA and FA 1981.

Local authorities
S.127 & Sch.18

As a consequence of changes introduced by the Local Government Finance Act 1988 a new definition of a local authority for the purposes of their exemption from tax is necessary and is effective as of 1 April 1990. As far as England and Wales are concerned the definition also includes police and fire authorities.

APPENDIX

RATES AND ALLOWANCES 1990/91

Income tax	Taxable income bands	Rate	Tax on band
	£	%	£
	0 to 20,700	25	5,175
	Over 20,700	40	

	Allowances	£
	Personal allowance	3,005
	Married couple's allowance	1,720
	Blind person	1,080
	Widow's bereavement	1,720
	Additional personal allowance	1,720

	Persons aged 65 to 74	
	Personal allowance	3,670
	Married couple's allowance	2,145

	Persons aged 75 and over	
	Personal allowance	3,820
	Married couple's allowance	2,185
	Income limit for age allowance	12,300

Capital gains tax	*Annual exemptions*	£
	Individuals, personal representatives and trusts for disabled persons	5,000
	Other trusts	2,500

Inheritance tax	*Chargeable values from 6 April 1990 from*				*On death**
	£				*Rate %*
	0 to 128,000				Nil
	Over 128,000				40

* Includes transfers made within seven years of death with tapering relief on transfers between seven years and three years before death as follows:

Charge on gifts within seven years of death:

Intervening years	0-3	3-4	4-5	5-6	6-7
% of full charge	100	80	60	40	20

Chargeable lifetime transfers which are not potentially exempt transfers are charged at half the full rate but additional tax may become payable by reference to the full rate if the transferor dies within seven years of making the gift.

Car and fuel benefits		*Car benefit*		*Fuel benefit*
		Under four years old	*Four years old or more*	
		£	£	£
	Car costing up to £19,250			
	1400 cc or less	1,700	1,150	480
	1401 cc to 2000 cc	2,200	1,500	600
	Over 2000 cc	3,550	2,350	900
	Car costing from £19,251 to £29,000			
	All cars	4,600	3,100	
	Car costing over £29,000			
	All cars	7,400	4,900	

Car and fuel benefits are reduced by half for a car used for 18,000 or more business miles per annum.

Car benefit but not fuel benefit is increased by half for a second car or a car used for less than 2,500 business miles per annum.

Pension contribution limits	Personal pension schemes		Retirement annuity premiums	
	Age on 6 April	*% NRE**	*Age on 6 April*	*% NRE**
	35 or less	17.5	50 or less	17.5
	36 to 45	20	51 to 55	20
	46 to 50	25	56 to 60	22.5
	51 to 55	30	61 or over	27.5
	56 to 60	35		
	61 or over	40		

* Net relevant earnings

Corporation tax rates

	Financial year commencing 1 April 1990
Full rate	35%
Small companies' rate	25%
Small companies' fraction	1/40
Marginal rate	37½%
ACT rate (from 6 April 1990)	1/3

Small companies' rate applies if profits do not exceed £200,000. Between £200,000 and £1,000,000 marginal rates apply.

Value added tax

Standard rate	15%
	(3/23 VAT inclusive price)
Registration level from 20 March 1990	£25,400 pa
Deregistration limit	£24,400 pa

ERNST & YOUNG OFFICES IN THE UNITED KINGDOM

ABERDEEN	50 Huntly Street, Aberdeen AB9 1XN, Tel: 0224 640033
BELFAST	Bedford House, 16 Bedford Street, Belfast BT2 7DT, Tel: 0232 246525
BIDEFORD	27 Bridgeland Street, Bideford, North Devon EX39 2PZ, Tel: 0237 471881
BIRMINGHAM	PO Box 1, 3 Colmore Row, Birmingham B3 2DB, Tel: 021-626 6262
BRADFORD	Clifton House, 2 Clifton Villas, Bradford BD8 7DW, Tel: 0274 498153
BRISTOL	One Bridewell Street, Bristol BS1 2AA, Tel: 0272 290808
CAMBRIDGE	Compass House, 80 Newmarket Road, Cambridge CB5 8DZ, Tel: 0223 461200
CARDIFF	Pendragon House, Fitzalan Court, Fitzalan Road, Cardiff CF2 1TF, Tel: 0222 484641
DUNDEE	City House, 16 Overgate, Dundee DD1 9PN, Tel: 0382 202561
EDINBURGH	17 Abercromby Place, Edinburgh EH3 6LT, Tel: 031-556 8641
EXETER	Broadwalk House, Southernhay West, Exeter EX1 1LF, Tel: 0392 433541
FORFAR	Manor Street, Forfar, Angus DD8 1EX, Tel: 0307 62516
GLASGOW	George House, 50 George Square, Glasgow G2 1RR, Tel: 041-552 3456
HULL	PO Box 3, Lowgate House, Lowgate, Hull HU1 1JJ, Tel: 0482 25531
INVERNESS	Moray House, 16 Bank Street, Inverness IV1 1QY, Tel: 0463 237581
IPSWICH	Queens House, Queen Street, Ipswich IP1 1SW, Tel: 0473 217491
LEEDS	PO Box 61, Cloth Hall Court, 14 King Street, Leeds LS1 2JN, Tel: 0532 431221
LEICESTER	Provincial House, 37 New Walk, Leicester LE1 6TU, Tel: 0533 549818
LIVERPOOL	Silkhouse Court, Tithebarn Street, Liverpool L2 2LE, Tel: 051-236 8214
LONDON	Becket House, 1 Lambeth Palace Road, London SE1 7EU, Tel: 071-928 2000
	Rolls House, 7 Rolls Buildings, Fetter Lane, London EC4A 1NH, Tel: 071-928 2000
LUTON	65 Park Street, Luton LU1 3JX, Tel: 0582 454411
MANCHESTER	Commercial Union House, Albert Square, Manchester M2 6LP, Tel: 061-953 9000
MILTON KEYNES	380 Silbury Court, Silbury Boulevard, Central Milton Keynes MK9 2AF, Tel: 0908 672882
NEWCASTLE UPON TYNE	Norham House, 12 New Bridge Street West, Newcastle upon Tyne NE1 8AD, Tel: 091-261 1063
NORWICH	Cambridge House, 26 Tombland, Norwich NR3 1RH, Tel: 0603 660482
NOTTINGHAM	10-12 The Ropewalk, Nottingham NG1 5DT, Tel: 0602 411861
PERTH	2-4 Blackfriars Street, Perth PH1 5NB, Tel: 0738 33551
PETERBOROUGH	New Priestgate House, 57 Priestgate, Peterborough PE1 1JX, Tel: 0733 60348
PLYMOUTH	St Andrew's Court, Notte Street, Plymouth PL1 2AH, Tel: 0752 673567
READING	Apex Plaza, Reading RG1 1YE, Tel: 0734 500611
SHEFFIELD	Talbot Chambers, 2-6 North Church Street, Sheffield S1 2DH, Tel: 0742 752929
SOUTHAMPTON	Wessex House, 19 Threefield Lane, Southampton SO1 1TW, Tel: 0703 230230
SWINDON	Old Town Court, 10-14 High Street, Swindon SN1 3EP, Tel: 0793 618822
TELFORD	Fuller House, Hall Court, Hall Park Way, Telford TF3 4NG, Tel: 0952 291575
TORQUAY	Commerce House, Abbey Road, Torquay TQ2 5RU, Tel: 0803 213013